OXFORD
UNIVERSITY PRESS

Blackstone's Police Sergeants' and Inspectors' Mock Examination Paper 2025

Pack 1

Contents

OXFORD
UNIVERSITY PRESS

Great Clarendon Street, Oxford, OX2 6DP,
United Kingdom

Oxford University Press is a department of the University of Oxford.
It furthers the University's objective of excellence in research, scholarship,
and education by publishing worldwide. Oxford is a registered trade mark of
Oxford University Press in the UK and in certain other countries

First Edition published in 2004
Twenty-first Edition published in 2024

Published in the United States of America by Oxford University Press
198 Madison Avenue, New York, NY 10016, United States of America

British Library Cataloguing in Publication Data
Data available

Library of Congress Control Number
Data available

ISBN 978–0–19–893600–8

Printed in the UK by
Bell & Bain Ltd., Glasgow

Acknowledgements

I would like to thank all the team at Oxford University Press for their continued and highly professional support and assistance in the production of this product.

Above all, I thank my wife, Kate, for giving me the utmost encouragement and self-belief without which none of this would ever have happened.

Paul Connor

Introduction to the Mock Examination

Every single MCQ (multiple-choice question) in this mock examination is based on the syllabuses for the sergeants' and inspectors' examinations of 2025.

Whilst this mock exam offers a useful means to test your knowledge and understanding of the police promotion examination syllabus, the content itself should not be considered indicative of the 'live' examination. Each MCQ has been created from relevant material contained in the three-volume Blackstone's Police Manuals for 2025 (*Crime*, *Evidence and Procedure* and *General Police Duties*). These Manuals are the basis for both of the police promotion examinations that will take place in 2025. As a result, **whatever police promotion examination you are taking**, you can be sure that each MCQ in this mock examination is a valid test of your knowledge and understanding of the law as all of the MCQs will directly relate to the material that you have studied for the examination.

'How can this mock examination be suitable for ***both*** *sets of candidates?'*

It is important to highlight that the material studied by sergeants' and inspectors' candidates is **exactly the same** apart from the exclusion of the chapter dealing with Weapons (from the *Crime Manual*) from the inspectors' examination.

In order to make this examination relevant to both sets of candidates, there will be no MCQs asked on that chapter. At this point, sergeants' candidates may think that the examination is less relevant to them; but this is not so.

My analysis of the last 12 sergeants' examinations shows that the excluded Weapons chapter was worth an average of three to four MCQs per examination. Not being questioned on that solitary chapter does not make this examination any less valuable to the sergeants' candidates as it represents a small part of the examination process for sergeants' candidates. As you will discover, the scope of the examination is still huge and I have managed to cover a great many subjects within the 150 MCQs.

As the range of the three Manuals is significant, I have set MCQs across a broad spectrum of the syllabuses; this makes the examination as fair a test of your overall knowledge and understanding as is possible. Some areas that have, historically, been allocated several MCQs in the exams have been treated in the same way in this mock, e.g. '*Public Order Offences*' and '*Theft & Related Offences*'. This means that the mock examination is a reasonable reflection of the content of the Manuals.

A by-product of this approach is that some of the MCQs in the mock examination may appear to relate to obscure or rarely used pieces of legislation. Historically, this is the source of many candidate complaints about the examination proper and the reason for the often heard criticism, '*It's not based on reality*', which has been levelled year after year at the police promotion examination process. What candidates have to accept is that the examination is not about the 'reality' of day-to-day policing; it is a test of an individual's knowledge and understanding of the law contained in the syllabuses. These MCQs should not be treated with contempt just because a candidate has never dealt with a particular offence or feels that it is unimportant; any such approach would be unwise. Remember that the police promotion examinations are based on the sergeants' and inspectors' syllabuses and therefore everything contained within those syllabuses is potentially testable.

From March 2023, MCQs in your examination are presented in the order of the three Manuals (although not in chapter order). Mirroring that exam structure means that you will begin this mock by answering 60 randomly ordered MCQs on Crime, followed by 32 randomly ordered MCQs on Evidence and Procedure and finally 58 MCQs on General Police Duties.

Importantly, the structure of the MCQs in the mock examination matches the structure of MCQs that you will face in the examination proper. You cannot accurately assess your knowledge, understanding and application of the law if you are not testing it in the same way as you will be tested in your examination.

The style of MCQs you will face in your police promotion examination will mirror the following:

> BREEN plans an armed robbery on a security van that regularly picks up cash at a local bank. He enlists the help of FISH and TODD who agree to actually carry out the armed robbery while BREEN waits for them at a rendezvous point. BREEN has no intention of taking part in the commission of the armed robbery itself. Unknown to BREEN, the security company has been 'tipped off' about the robbery and changes the day of collection so that the security van does not arrive at the bank. FISH and TODD leave empty-handed.
>
> Does BREEN commit statutory conspiracy contrary to s. 1 of the Criminal Law Act 1977?
>
> **A** No, BREEN has no intention of taking part in the actual armed robbery itself.
> **B** Yes, BREEN commits the offence as soon as he plans the robbery and before he enlists the help of FISH and TODD.
> **C** No, the commission of the offence is impossible because the security van would never arrive at the bank.
> **D** Yes, BREEN has agreed on a course of conduct that will involve the commission of an offence.

One minor point to make regarding the above format is that exam MCQs do not have an 'A', 'B', 'C' or 'D' next to each option as you will be taking the exam online and click on the choice you make which is highlighted once you do so. As this is not possible with a paper exam, there is a requirement for the ABCD element to be included in the mock MCQs. Finally, you will notice when marking the mock examination that 10 MCQs will be excluded from the marking process—this replicates the marking process in your examination proper. In your examination, the 10 MCQs that perform poorest against a broad range of criteria (contrary to popular myth, *the sole criteria* these questions are judged against *is not* how many candidates answer the MCQ incorrectly) will be removed from the marking process. As analysing future candidate performance in relation to the 150 MCQs in this mock exam to obtain such data is not possible, 10 MCQs have been randomly selected to count as those 'poor performing' MCQs to ensure that you are marked out of 140 rather than 150 MCQs.

Now that you are familiar with how the mock examination has been produced and written, it is appropriate to consider the benefits of taking the examination: this is primarily to be able to assess your performance accurately. This can, in turn, help you in a number of ways:

1. It may highlight areas of weakness (e.g. your knowledge of General Police Duties may not be as good as you think it is).
2. It may highlight areas of strength (e.g. your knowledge of Crime may be stronger than you think it is).

A direct consequence of the previous two points is that the mock examination could help you channel your study/revision into more productive areas of your syllabus.

3. It is a good test of your ability to deal with 150 MCQs in a three-hour period. The pressure of dealing with an MCQ once every 72 seconds (the average time per question) can be intense. Will you be able to cope with it? Will you have to take steps to increase the pace of your MCQ answering in order to complete the exam proper? On the other hand, did you finish with a great deal of time to spare? If you manage the latter with this mock examination then you are doing exceptionally well as it would take the 'average' person approximately two hours and six minutes *just to read the text of the 150 MCQs*, let alone deal with the issues they raise regarding the law. That being the case, are you giving the MCQs enough thought before answering?

I cannot stress enough how important this benefit is. After every exam, I hear from officers who run out of time with 10, 20 or even more questions left to answer. These officers either have to guess the answers to those MCQs or do not even have the opportunity to do that. Whilst not necessarily fatal to the chances of success, you can imagine this is not a position you want to be in. I know it may be difficult to follow my instructions, i.e. to allocate three hours and stick to it, but I believe that this practice is invaluable. What a waste of your study/revision effort to fail not because of a lack of knowledge, but because your timekeeping was at fault.

4. Answering correctly structured MCQs is an excellent way to test your knowledge.
5. The preparation involved in a 'dry-run' full examination will assist in building your confidence to deal with the examination proper.
6. It will improve your exam technique by allowing you to see how easy it is to make a mistake, either by failing to read the question correctly or by reading too much into the question.

However you perform in the mock examination, I would strongly advise that you do not read too much into your result. Failing or passing this examination does not warrant despair or joy; this mock examination is primarily intended to give you practice and is not a predictor of performance in the examination proper.

I hope that your efforts are rewarded and wish you every success in your 2025 police promotion examination.

Paul Connor

Instructions for Completion

READ THE WHOLE OF THE INSTRUCTIONS BEFORE ATTEMPTING THE MOCK EXAMINATION

If you want to get the most from this mock examination, then you must treat it as if you were sitting the examination in paper form.

Time

You have up to three hours to complete the examination. It might not take you that long but it is best to assume that it will, so please make absolutely sure that you set aside three hours. You cannot expect to sit part of the examination for one hour, take a break for 20 minutes, return to the examination and then get an accurate picture of your performance. The examination must be completed in one three-hour sitting. However, if you have been allocated extra time to take the examination (for example, you may have been provided with reasonable adjustments because you are dyslexic), add that time to the standard three-hour examination time frame and if that includes breaks, take them—the idea is that the mock exam is taken in the same circumstances as you would take the examination proper.

Environment

You need to be able to concentrate on the examination and you cannot do that if the television is on, the phone is ringing etc. Find a place where you will not be disturbed for the duration of this examination and make sure that there are no distractions that will affect your performance.

Equipment

Ideally you will sit at a desk to take the mock examination. Trying to fill out the answer sheet on your lap whilst holding the question paper open will prove to be a difficult task to say the least. Make sure that you can see a clock, stopwatch or wristwatch.

You will need two pencils, a pencil sharpener and an eraser.

If you require any other materials in relation to reasonable adjustments, ensure they are available to you.

Pack 1

In Pack 1, you will find a blank answer sheet and the question booklet. Place both documents on the table.

When you decide to start the examination, please open the question booklet. Work through the test MCQs and make your choice of A, B, C or D by putting a horizontal line through the corresponding letter on the answer sheet.

Only mark one answer for each question.

Make sure that if you change your answer you erase the previous mark fully.

Try not to leave blank answers when you are unsure. Mark an answer and come back to the question if you have time at the end of the examination.

Pack 2

When you have finished the examination, open Pack 2 and begin the marking process. When you have finished marking your paper, please refer to the answer booklet for a detailed explanation of the correct answers with paragraph references to the *Blackstone's Police Manuals 2025*.

The marking process will take some time—to ensure accuracy, please do not rush this stage!

OXFORD
UNIVERSITY PRESS

Blackstone's Police Sergeants' and Inspectors' Mock Examination Paper 2025

Question Booklet

Time Allowed—180 minutes

1. Each of the questions is followed by four possible answers, only ONE of which is correct. Choose the ONE response that you consider to be correct. On the answer sheet, mark the box that corresponds to your selection. Mark your answer clearly with a — mark. The answer sheet has spaces for your answers to all questions. If you change your mind about an answer, rub out the first mark, then mark your new answer. Mark only one answer for each question.
2. You are reminded that there is no need to read the whole examination paper before beginning to select answers to the questions posed.
3. You must ensure that BEFORE the close of the examination, all of your answers to the questions have been correctly entered on the answer sheet.
4. You may make any notes you wish on the question papers.

1. DAVENPORT is planning to carry out a robbery at a post office and decides to use an air rifle during the offence as a means to threaten and frighten staff at the post office into doing as he demands. DAVENPORT is convinced that the police are tracking his movements and wants to minimise the risk of his arrest and prosecution so he uses his 14-year-old nephew, KIRVELL, to take the air rifle to a garage at the rear of the post office and hide it next to several large bins. DAVENPORT's plan is to make sure he is not followed to the post office and, once he is happy that that is the case, he will go to the bins, recover the air rifle and commit the robbery.

   With regard to the offence of using someone to mind a weapon (contrary to s. 28(1) of the Violent Crime Reduction Act 2006), at what stage, if at all, has an offence first been committed by DAVENPORT?

   A No offence is committed by DAVENPORT as 'weapons' do not include firearms.
   B No offence is committed by DAVENPORT as the activity took place with an air weapon and this is not a 'dangerous weapon'.
   C The offence is first committed when DAVENPORT uses KIRVELL to transport the air rifle to the rear of the post office.
   D The offence is first committed when DAVENPORT uses KIRVELL to hide the air rifle next to several large bins.

2. BRADLEY and WITHERSTON meet at a party and in conversation they find out that they both have an interest in sadomasochistic sexual activities. They agree to meet at BRADLEY's house where they will have sexual intercourse and engage in sadomasochistic activities where they will cause serious injury to each other for the purposes of obtaining sexual gratification. The pair meet at BRADLEY's home the following day and they have sexual intercourse. During the sexual intercourse, WITHERSTON tells BRADLEY to punch him in the face; BRADLEY does and causes WITHERSTON to temporarily lose consciousness (a s. 47 Offences Against the Person Act 1861 offence). WITHERSTON regains consciousness and tells BRADLEY to hit him much harder; BRADLEY does so and breaks WITHERSTON's jaw (a s. 20 Offences Against the Person Act 1861 offence). BRADLEY screams *'Do the same to me!'* and, intending to cause BRADLEY serious injury, WITHERSTON hits her in the face and breaks her jaw (a s. 18 Offences Against the Person Act 1861 offence).

   At what stage, if at all, would the provisions of s. 71(2) of the Domestic Abuse Act 2021 (consenting to serious harm for the purposes of sexual gratification) first be relevant to the offence committed?

   A Section 71(2) would be irrelevant to this scenario.
   B When the s. 47 offence is committed.
   C When the s. 20 offence is committed.
   D When the s. 18 offence is committed.

3. STEWART is looking out of the window of her flat and can see a car parked on a private car park used solely by residents of the block of flats she lives in. She can see BRADY (who is a resident of the flats) sitting in the driver's seat of the car and watches a number of people approach him and exchanges of some type take place; STEWART forms the opinion that BRADY is dealing drugs. She contacts the police and PC JONES, on uniform mobile patrol, attends the scene. PC JONES speaks to BRADY and because of his responses to questions and the information from STEWART, the officer forms the suspicion that BRADY is in possession of a controlled drug and also suspects that controlled drugs may be found in the car. The officer is considering using the power under s. 23(2) of the Misuse of Drugs Act 1971 to search BRADY and the car he is sitting in.

   Considering the powers of entry, search and seizure under s. 23(2) of the Misuse of Drugs Act 1971, which of the following comments is correct?

   A PC JONES cannot use the power; it requires the officer to have reasonable grounds to believe that a person is in possession of controlled drugs in contravention of the Act.
   B PC JONES can use the power but will only be able to search BRADY for controlled drugs.
   C PC JONES cannot use the power in a private car park.
   D PC JONES can use the power and will be able to search BRADY and the car for controlled drugs.

4. HENDRIE attacks COPEMAN in a street and fractures COPEMAN's skull. COPEMAN is rushed to hospital where an examination of COPEMAN shows that the fractured skull has caused brain damage. The seriousness of COPEMAN's situation is compounded by the fact that it is discovered that he has a serious stomach ulcer. The brain damage keeps COPEMAN in a coma and prevents doctors from operating on the stomach ulcer. One month later, the ulcer bursts and causes COPEMAN to die.

   Considering concepts associated with criminal conduct and in particular the 'chain of causation', is HENDRIE liable for the death of COPEMAN?

   A Yes, but for HENDRIE's attack on COPEMAN, the ulcer could have been operated on and COPEMAN would not have died.
   B Yes, COPEMAN's death was a direct consequence of the assault by HENDRIE and, as the chain of causation can never be broken, HENDRIE is liable for COPEMAN's death.
   C No, because of the time delay between the discovery of the ulcer and COPEMAN's death.
   D No, because the untreated ulcer, not the fractured skull, was the cause of COPEMAN's death.

5. HAMILTON is eight months pregnant and out shopping in a town centre. She is approached by WINDEBANK who, in an unprovoked attack, stabs HAMILTON in the stomach several times. HAMILTON is seriously injured and is rushed to hospital and, as a result of the attack, gives premature birth to her child. The child is born alive but dies five days after being born and as a direct consequence of the injuries received during the attack by WINDEBANK on HAMILTON.

Which of the following statements correctly summarises WINDEBANK's liability in relation to the death of the child?

A WINDEBANK could be charged with the murder of the child if it can be proved that he intended to kill HAMILTON.
B WINDEBANK could only ever be charged with the manslaughter of the child.
C WINDEBANK could be charged with the murder of the child if it can be proved that he intended the child to die having been born alive.
D WINDEBANK could be charged with the murder of the child if it can be proved that he intended to kill or cause grievous bodily harm to HAMILTON.

6. JACKSON kidnaps DOYLE and takes him to a secluded house where he imprisons him in a cellar. JACKSON threatens to kill DOYLE unless he complies with his requests in relation to sexual activity. He points a pistol at DOYLE and gives DOYLE a dildo and tells DOYLE to place it in his (DOYLE's) mouth and simulate oral sex; DOYLE does so. JACKSON then demands that DOYLE place his (DOYLE's) penis in his (JACKSON's) mouth so that JACKSON can give DOYLE oral sex; DOYLE is terrified and agrees and DOYLE places his penis in JACKSON's mouth. JACKSON then tells DOYLE to open his mouth and, when he does so, JACKSON places his penis in DOYLE's mouth.

At what stage, if at all, does an offence of assault by penetration (contrary to s. 2 of the Sexual Offences Act 2003) first take place?

A When DOYLE is forced to simulate oral sex with a dildo.
B When DOYLE is forced to place his penis in JACKSON's mouth.
C When JACKSON places his penis in DOYLE's mouth.
D The offence has not been committed in these circumstances.

7. PC GINN attends a house where it is reported that CAMPBELL (a child aged 16) has been suffering ill-treatment and neglect at the hands of her foster-parent. PC GINN sees CAMPBELL and speaks to her and concludes that the allegations appear to be true. Believing that CAMPBELL would otherwise be likely to suffer significant harm, the officer uses the powers under s. 46 of the Children Act 1989 and takes CAMPBELL into 'police protection'.

   Is this a lawful use of the powers available under s. 46 of the Children Act 1989?

   A No, as CAMPBELL is 16 years old.
   B Yes, but the maximum period of time CAMPBELL could spend in 'police protection' is 72 hours.
   C No, an officer of the rank of inspector or above must authorise the use of the power.
   D Yes, and PC GINN can also carry out the role of the 'designated officer' in these circumstances.

8. ROSE is lying on a sun lounger in her private rear garden, wearing a bikini and sunbathing. SHUTER, who is ROSE's next-door neighbour, sees ROSE and is outraged by her behaviour as she believes ROSE is trying to seduce her husband and that this activity is part of a bigger plan. She leans over the fence separating the rear gardens and shouts *'Whore!'* at ROSE. ROSE thinks SHUTER is an idiot and, intending to cause SHUTER alarm and distress, she rips off her bikini top and exposes her breasts to SHUTER. She immediately follows this act by standing up, pulling her bikini pants down and exposing her buttocks ('mooning') to SHUTER shouting *'Kiss my arse, you silly old bag!'*

   Does ROSE commit an offence of exposure (contrary to s. 66 of the Sexual Offences Act 1968)?

   A No, as this offence requires the activity to be carried out for the purposes of sexual gratification rather than to cause alarm or distress.
   B Yes, exposing the buttocks and the female breasts with intent to cause alarm or distress would amount to an offence.
   C No, as ROSE did not expose her genitals to SHUTER.
   D Yes, although the buttocks are not included, exposing the female breasts with intent to cause alarm or distress amounts to an offence.

9. In the early hours of the morning, MINCHER and his wife are asleep in an upstairs bedroom of their house when they are woken by a noise from the downstairs living room. MINCHER is petrified that this is a burglar and grabs hold of the first thing to hand, in this case a golf club, to protect himself and his wife. Moments later, BARBER bursts into the bedroom. Only thinking about protecting his wife, MINCHER lashes out towards BARBER with the golf club. The club strikes BARBER on the shoulder and he falls to the floor. BARBER shouts out, *'You'll pay for that, pal!'* and starts to get up, at which point MINCHER, honestly believing it is necessary to do so, strikes BARBER on the head with the golf club. This causes BARBER severe injury leading to him being in a permanent vegetative state.

   Would MINCHER's use of force be considered legitimate in these circumstances?

   A Yes, the use of even grossly disproportionate force can be justified in 'householder' cases.
   B No, as MINCHER was acting to protect his wife and not himself.
   C Yes, the use of disproportionate force can be regarded as reasonable in 'householder' cases.
   D No, as the use of disproportionate force cannot be justified in any circumstances.

10. PC VINCENT is on uniform foot patrol during which he lawfully stops and searches RAFFIN under s. 23 of the Misuse of Drugs Act 1971. During the course of the search, PC VINCENT finds a substantial quantity of what he suspects to be cannabis resin in a bag that RAFFIN is carrying. When PC VINCENT finds the drug, RAFFIN says, *'It's cannabis resin, you might as well nick me.'* RAFFIN is arrested by PC VINCENT and later that day RAFFIN's home address is searched. During the search, a quantity of khat (leaves of the plant) is found in the living room of the house along with documentation showing that RAFFIN has ordered a quantity of cannabis seeds to be delivered by post to his house. In interview, RAFFIN states that he knew the cannabis was in his bag, that he had khat leaves in his house and had ordered cannabis seeds to be delivered by post.

   Considering the classification of and 'possession' of controlled drugs, which of the following comments is correct?

   A RAFFIN is in possession of the cannabis found in his bag and the khat leaves in the living room of his house.
   B The only drug RAFFIN is in possession of is the cannabis found in his bag during the s. 23 search.
   C RAFFIN is in possession of drugs in relation to the cannabis in his bag and the cannabis seeds he has ordered to be delivered by post.
   D RAFFIN is in possession of drugs in relation to the cannabis in his bag, the khat leaves in the living room of his house and the cannabis seeds he has ordered to be delivered by post.

11. WEBB breaks into a factory to steal anything of value. He is searching an office inside the factory when he is disturbed by GEORGE and PEACH (security guards working at the factory). WEBB picks up the first thing to hand which is a letter opener (not intending to steal it but to use it to threaten the security guards and cause them injury if necessary). He points the letter opener towards both guards and shouts *'Back off!'* but they start to walk towards him. Intending to cause GEORGE serious injury (as he is the closer of the two security guards), WEBB throws the letter opener at GEORGE—GEORGE dodges the letter opener but it hits PEACH in the eye causing him to lose his eye as a result (a really serious injury).

When does WEBB first commit an offence of aggravated burglary (contrary to s. 10 of the Theft Act 1968) in these circumstances?

A As soon as he arms himself with the letter opener.
B When he points the letter opener towards the security guards.
C When he throws the letter opener at GEORGE.
D When he causes serious injury to PEACH instead of GEORGE.

12. LOVE and PREHN are drinking in a pub when they become involved in a dispute about football. LOVE is annoyed at PREHN and swings his fist at PREHN intending to punch him in the face and injure him. LOVE does not intend to cause serious injury to PREHN but does appreciate that if the blow lands then it will cause some harm to PREHN. PREHN sees the blow coming and, believing he is going to be harmed, he ducks and LOVE misses him. However, LOVE's momentum carries him forward and the punch aimed at PREHN strikes CLARKE (who was standing behind PREHN) in the face. The blow to CLARKE's face breaks CLARKE's jaw.

Considering offences relating to attempts, assault and the doctrine of transferred *mens rea*, which of the following comments is correct?

A LOVE has committed an offence of s. 39 assault (contrary to the Criminal Justice Act 1988) against PREHN and an offence of s. 20 grievous bodily harm (contrary to the Offences Against the Person Act 1861) against CLARKE.
B LOVE has committed an offence of attempted battery (contrary to s. 1 of the Criminal Attempts Act 1981) against PREHN and an offence of s. 20 grievous bodily harm (contrary to the Offences Against the Person Act 1861) against CLARKE.
C LOVE has committed an offence of s. 39 assault (contrary to the Criminal Justice Act 1988) against PREHN and an offence of s. 18 grievous bodily harm (contrary to the Offences Against the Person Act 1861) against CLARKE.
D LOVE has committed an offence of s. 39 assault (contrary to the Criminal Justice Act 1988) against PREHN but is not liable for any offence in relation to the injury caused to CLARKE.

13. PHILLIPS is applying for a mortgage to purchase his first house. He earns £37,000 a year but realises that this will not be quite enough to obtain the mortgage he requires to purchase the house so falsifies information in the mortgage application and makes it appear that he is earning £45,000 a year. He submits the mortgage application to his bank which later discovers that PHILLIPS has lied on the mortgage application.

In relation to the offence of false accounting (contrary to s. 17 of the Theft Act 1968), which of the comments below is correct?

A No offence has been committed as the dishonest mortgage application was discovered and there was no 'gain or loss in money or other property' as a result.
B The offence has been committed by PHILLIPS as a mortgage application has been held to be a document required for an accounting purpose.
C No offence has been committed as PHILLIPS did not destroy, deface or conceal any account required for an accounting purpose.
D The offence has been committed but in order to prove the offence the prosecution will be required to prove an intention to permanently deprive by PHILLIPS.

14. BRADSHAW and ABEL work in the same office but do not get on with each other. BRADSHAW tampers with ABEL's office chair so that when ABEL sits on it, the back of the chair will give way causing ABEL to fall on the floor. BRADSHAW realises that this may cause some harm to ABEL but considers the risk to be a reasonable one as any harm will only be slight (perhaps some minor bruising). ABEL sits on the chair, falls off and breaks his arm. BRADSHAW is charged with a s. 20 offence (contrary to the Offences Against the Person Act 1861).

Considering the issues surrounding the concept of recklessness as they apply to the s. 20 offence, which of the following statements is correct?

A BRADSHAW is not 'reckless' for the purposes of this offence as he did not foresee the risk that serious harm would be caused to ABEL.
B Whether BRADSHAW was 'reckless' or not will be considered by the court/jury asking whether a reasonable bystander would have been aware of the risk of some injury being caused to ABEL.
C BRADSHAW is 'reckless' for the purposes of the s. 20 offence as he foresaw the risk that some harm would befall ABEL.
D As BRADSHAW considered the risk a reasonable one, he will not be 'reckless'.

15. HARRIS (a police officer) and INGLEBY (a nurse working in the Accident and Emergency ward of a hospital) are both off duty and have met to have a coffee in a cafe. A fight occurs in the cafe where O'TOOLE hits BENT in the face with a glass causing serious injury to BENT. O'TOOLE is about to make off but is stopped by HARRIS who identifies himself as a police officer and lawfully detains O'TOOLE who strikes the officer in the face committing actual bodily harm to the officer (contrary to s. 47 of the Offences Against the Person Act 1861). While INGLEBY is attending to BENT, BENT kicks out causing minor bruising (a s. 39 battery contrary to the Criminal Justice Act 1988) to INGLEBY.

    In relation to the Assaults on Emergency Workers (Offences) Act 2018, which of the following comments is correct?

    A The legislation is irrelevant in relation to both offences as HARRIS and INGLEBY were not 'on duty'.
    B The s. 39 battery against INGLEBY will be aggravated and thereby increase the potential maximum sentence for the offence; the fact that the s. 47 actual bodily harm was committed on an 'emergency worker' (HARRIS) is an aggravating factor increasing the seriousness of the offence.
    C The s. 47 actual bodily harm against HARRIS will be aggravated as it was committed against a police officer; INGLEBY (an off-duty nurse) is not an 'emergency worker' for the purposes of the Act.
    D The s. 39 battery against INGLEBY will be aggravated under the Act; the s. 47 actual bodily harm against HARRIS will not be aggravated and is irrelevant as far as the seriousness of the offence is concerned.

16. MATTHEWS is arrested, charged and later convicted at Crown Court of an offence of supplying a controlled drug (contrary s. 4(3) of the Misuse of Drugs Act 1971). The court sentences MATTHEWS to a single sentence period of three years' imprisonment.

    In respect of travel restriction orders under the Criminal Justice and Police Act 2001, which of the following comments is correct?

    A The court is under a duty to consider whether or not a travel restriction order would be appropriate.
    B A travel restriction order would not be relevant to this situation as MATTHEWS has only been sentenced to a period of imprisonment of three years.
    C A travel restriction order is appropriate and would last for a minimum period of four years.
    D A travel restriction order would not be relevant to this situation as MATTHEWS has not been convicted of a 'drug trafficking' offence.

17. RENDER is shopping in a retail park and buys several packs of needles from a craft shop. RENDER intends to insert the needles into some apples he has at his home address and place the apples in a supermarket to cause public alarm and anxiety. He returns to his home and inserts needles into a dozen apples. He puts the contaminated apples into a bag and takes them to a supermarket near to his home; the supermarket sells various goods including apples. He enters the supermarket and is looking for an opportunity to place the apples down without being seen. He is standing in a deserted aisle stocked with computer games and, seeing his opportunity, he places the apples next to a display of computer games.

Considering the offence of contaminating or interfering with goods (contrary to s. 38(1) of the Public Order Act 1986), which of the following comments is correct?

A RENDER commits an offence when he purchases the needles to contaminate the apples.
B When RENDER contaminates the apples with needles at his home address, he commits no offence (because he is at his place of abode at that time).
C RENDER did not commit an offence when he placed the contaminated apples in the computer games aisle (that is not a place where goods of that description are sold).
D RENDER commits an offence as he has contaminated 'natural' goods (the apples); the offence would not be committed if the contaminated goods were 'manufactured'.

18. PIGGOTT, SHERLOCK and BLOWER are chatting in a pub. The three have strong views about religion as they are all committed atheists. During the course of their conversation, they make several comments to the effect that 'there is no God or Gods'. These comments are overheard by TRAYLING who is a devout Christian and is deeply offended by the comments PIGGOTT, SHERLOCK and BLOWER have made. Enraged by their comments and motivated by his hostility towards atheists, TRAYLING picks up a chair and throws it at the group, intending to cause all three men very serious injury. As it happens, this only causes minor bruising to PIGGOTT (a s. 39 battery (Criminal Justice Act 1988)), a momentary loss of consciousness to SHERLOCK (a s. 47 actual bodily harm offence (Offences Against the Person Act 1861)) but it does break BLOWER's right arm (a s. 18 GBH offence (Offences Against the Person Act 1861)).

Considering the law regarding racially and religiously aggravated offences (under the Crime and Disorder Act 1998), which of the following comments is correct?

A A religiously aggravated offence has been committed against PIGGOTT and SHERLOCK but not against BLOWER.
B A religiously aggravated offence has been committed against SHERLOCK and BLOWER but not against PIGGOTT.
C A religiously aggravated offence has been committed against PIGGOTT but not against SHERLOCK or BLOWER.
D None of the assault offences would be religiously aggravated in these circumstances.

19. SIMPSON wants to carry out a robbery at a bank but is very much aware that he will need assistance to carry out the offence. He believes that a work colleague, FLAVELL, will help him commit the offence and approaches him in the workplace and suggests the robbery to FLAVELL, intending to encourage FLAVELL to take part in the robbery offence. FLAVELL tells SIMPSON he is an idiot and to go away. SIMPSON knows FLAVELL is a cocaine addict so offers to fund his cocaine habit for a month if he joins in with the robbery. FLAVELL agrees but states he will only carry out the robbery if the cocaine is provided in advance; SIMPSON agrees and supplies FLAVELL with a large amount of cocaine. The fact is that FLAVELL has no intention whatsoever of going through with the offence and consequently the robbery never actually occurs.

Which of the following comments is correct in relation to the offence of encouraging or assisting an offence (contrary to s. 44 of the Serious Crime Act 2007)?

A SIMPSON commits the offence when he initially puts his idea to FLAVELL in the workplace.
B SIMPSON commits the offence but this does not happen until he offers cocaine to FLAVELL and FLAVELL agrees to commit the robbery.
C The offence is not committed as FLAVELL never forms an intention of carrying out the robbery offence.
D The offence is not committed as the robbery never actually occurs.

20. RIMMER is driving a Vauxhall Astra along a road in an erratic manner. DC HALL (dressed in plain clothes and driving an unmarked police vehicle) is behind RIMMER and witnesses the poor driving. RIMMER reaches a set of traffic lights and stops his vehicle. DC HALL gets out of his vehicle and approaches RIMMER. He identifies himself as a police officer and speaks to RIMMER. RIMMER's responses are slurred and DC HALL forms the opinion that he is unfit to drive and arrests RIMMER for the offence of driving whilst unfit (contrary to s. 4(1) of the Road Traffic Act 1988). DC HALL reaches through the car door to take hold of RIMMER; RIMMER has no intention of allowing the officer to arrest and detain him so he slams the car door on the officer's arm, breaking DC HALL's arm in the process. RIMMER did not intend to break the officer's arm, just to stop the officer arresting him, although he did realise that slamming the door on the officer's arm would cause some harm to the officer.

Considering the liability of RIMMER in relation to offences against the person, which of the comments below is correct?

A RIMMER is not liable for any offence as the arrest the officer made was unlawful.
B RIMMER has committed a s. 47 battery offence.
C RIMMER has committed a s. 20 grievous bodily harm offence.
D RIMMER has committed a s. 18 grievous bodily harm offence.

21. JUDGE works as a clerk for a large car sales firm. She is examining a number of expenses claims (required for accounting purposes) that have been submitted by WILSON (a supervisor at the car sales firm). JUDGE discovers a significant number of irregularities suggesting that expenses amounting to £3,000 are false and she confronts WILSON regarding the irregularities. WILSON admits the expenses are false but threatens JUDGE to the effect that if she does anything about the false claims he will make sure that she loses her job, and he tells JUDGE to falsify the expenses claims so that they appear genuine. WILSON has a great deal of influence at the firm and JUDGE honestly believes he could get her sacked. JUDGE fears that this loss of income will have a dramatic impact on her standard of living and she falsifies the expenses for WILSON.

Would JUDGE be able to claim that she was acting under duress of circumstances in relation to any offences that she commits by falsifying the expenses claims?

A No, as she did not have cause to fear she that would suffer death or serious injury if she did not do as WILSON demanded.
B Yes, as the defence is available in answer to any charge except for treason.
C No, as duress of circumstances is only a defence to a charge of murder or attempted murder.
D Yes, because she honestly believed that she would be sacked if she did not do as WILSON demanded.

22. FULFORD breaks into an office used by 'Save the Children' (a large charity organisation) and steals several branded jackets and T-shirts that the charity fundraisers wear whilst trying to obtain charitable donations. FULFORD knows that McGREEVY, a criminal associate of FULFORD's, commits fraud offences by convincing people he is a charity collector and thinks the clothing could help him commit crime. FULFORD approaches McGREEVY and offers to sell the clothing to him intending that McGREEVY will use it to commit fraud offences. McGREEVY buys the clothing but never actually uses it as he is arrested that afternoon and the clothing found and seized by the police.

Does FULFORD commit an offence of making or supplying articles for use in fraud (contrary to s. 7 of the Fraud Act 2003)?

A No, as the clothing was never used to commit any offences of fraud.
B Yes, at the moment FULFORD offered to supply the clothing to McGREEVY.
C No, as FULFORD did not make or produce the clothing.
D Yes, at the moment McGREEVY buys the stolen clothing.

23. GRAHAM is a well-known drug dealer, primarily selling cocaine. He has £5,000 worth of cocaine hidden in his house when he is contacted by another drug dealer who tells GRAHAM that the police are carrying out a series of raids across the area and if he has any drugs he should move them. GRAHAM panics and thinks he needs to do something quickly about a potentially dangerous situation he might be in so he takes the £5,000 of cocaine to SULLIVAN (his neighbour) and says that if SULLIVAN looks after the drugs for a couple of days he will be paid £200. SULLIVAN is reluctant so GRAHAM offers him £500 which persuades SULLIVAN who takes the drugs from GRAHAM and looks after them for two days before returning the drugs to GRAHAM. SULLIVAN knows exactly what the drugs are and that returning them to GRAHAM means GRAHAM can sell the drugs for profit.

Who, if anyone at all, commits an offence of supplying a controlled drug (contrary to s. 4(3) of the Misuse of Drugs Act 1971)?

A The offence is not committed in these circumstances.
B Only GRAHAM.
C Only SULLIVAN.
D GRAHAM and SULLIVAN.

24. PC COLE is called to deal with a dispute at a car dealership where HUNT has bought a car and is complaining to LEE (the owner) about the quality of the vehicle and several mechanical issues with it. When the officer arrives at the scene, HUNT is shouting at LEE and demanding that he return the money that was paid for the car. PC COLE approaches HUNT and asks him to calm down so that he can establish what the situation is. HUNT looks at PC COLE and says *'Fuck me! A yank copper? Uncle Sam ain't telling me how to run my life pal!'* and punches the officer in the face causing minor bruising (a s. 39 battery contrary to the Criminal Justice Act 1988). PC COLE speaks with a strong American accent as he was born and lived in California for 25 years before moving to England five years ago, becoming a British citizen and then joining the police.

Does HUNT commit a racially aggravated assault offence (contrary to s. 29(1)(c) of the Crime and Disorder Act 1998)?

A No, as police officers cannot be 'victims' of a racially or religiously aggravated offence.
B No, as a s. 39 battery is not an offence that can become racially or religiously aggravated.
C Yes, if PC COLE perceives this to be a racist incident.
D Yes, as there has been a demonstration of racial hostility immediately before a relevant trigger offence.

25. ALI and ELDER are members of a gang who carry out offences of burglary. ALI and ELDER along with the gang leader, MILBURN, are carrying out a burglary at a warehouse when they are disturbed by a security guard. MILBURN tells ALI and ELDER to *'sort out'* the security guard by attacking him. The pair hesitate as they are not violent people. MILBURN says *'It's you two or him—kill him or I'll kill you both now!'* MILBURN has a violent past and so, believing they will be killed if they do not kill the security guard, they do as MILBURN demands. They attack the security guard and cause him life-threatening injuries—fortunately, the security guard survives. ALI and ELDER are later arrested and charged with the attempted murder of the security guard (ALI as a principal offender and ELDER as a secondary offender who aided the offence). Both state that they committed the offence under duress.

In relation to the defence of duress, which of the following comments is correct?

A The defence would not be available to either ALI or ELDER as they are charged with attempted murder.
B The defence would be available to ELDER (as a secondary offender) but not to ALI (the principal offender).
C The defence would be available to ALI and ELDER as they were threatened with death if they did not commit the offence.
D The defence would not be available as ALI and ELDER are part of a gang and the threat of death came from another gang member.

26. ASSENZA visits a country show with his family and parks his car on a makeshift car park situated within the grounds of the private estate where the country show is taking place. ASSENZA returns to his car several hours later and finds that his car has been blocked in by another car owned by MILEN. ASSENZA waits for 30 minutes but there is no sign of MILEN, so ASSENZA opens the door of MILEN's car, releases the handbrake and, standing outside the car, he pushes it 15 feet so that it no longer causes an obstruction. ASSENZA believes that he has the lawful authority to do so as MILEN's car was blocking his exit.

Would this constitute an offence of taking a conveyance (contrary to s. 12 of the Theft Act 1968)?

A No, the offence has not been committed as the activity took place on private land not a road or other public place.
B Yes, the offence has been committed but ASSENZA would have a defence as he believed that he had lawful authority to take the conveyance.
C No, the offence has not been committed as MILEN's car has not been used as a conveyance.
D Yes, the offence has been committed and ASSENZA would have no defence of 'lawful authority' as he is not a police officer, council worker or agent of a finance company repossessing a vehicle.

27. GRAY plans to rape SMITH. SMITH is an estate agent and GRAY's plan is to arrange a viewing of a house with her and once inside the house he will commit the offence. He phones SMITH's office and speaks to her saying that he is outside the house and is in a position to view it immediately if she can get to him as soon as possible. Keen to make a sale, SMITH leaves her office and drives to the house where she meets GRAY outside. She accompanies him into the house and has been showing him around for about 10 minutes when she becomes suspicious and decides to leave. GRAY realises he has been found out and stands in front of the front door preventing SMITH from leaving. SMITH punches GRAY in the face and manages to escape.

At what point, if at all, does GRAY first commit an offence of kidnapping (contrary to common law)?

A When he makes the phone call and lures SMITH to the house.
B When he accompanies her into the house under false pretences.
C When he stands in front of the front door preventing her from leaving.
D The offence has not been committed (GRAY did not use force to carry SMITH away).

28. Alec and Lily CHADWICK are married. The couple are always arguing because Lily believes that Alec is having an affair with one of his co-workers. One evening, Alec is several hours late home from work having worked overtime. When he arrives home, Lily is fuming and storms out of the house with a large container of white spirit which she throws over Alec's car. She sets light to the spirit and causes £4,000 worth of damage to Alec's car by fire (the car belongs solely to Alec). The police are called to the scene and Lily CHADWICK is arrested.

Which of the comments below is correct in relation to the prosecution of a charge of criminal damage (arson) and its mode of trial?

A As the damage done is less than £5,000, if Lily CHADWICK is tried for the offence this will take place in a magistrates' court.
B A prosecution for unlawful damage may only be instituted against Lily CHADWICK by or with the consent of the DPP.
C Because the offence is arson, it must be tried in the Crown Court.
D A prosecution for unlawful damage in such circumstances may only be instituted against Lily CHADWICK by or with the consent of the Attorney General.

29. SIMIC has acrimoniously split up with WALKER (his long-time girlfriend) and there is a nasty feud between them regarding access to their 6-month-old baby. SIMIC is chatting to a friend of his on a street corner when he sees WALKER walking towards him holding their baby in her arms. Seeing WALKER is too much for SIMIC, who loses his temper and runs up behind WALKER and grabs her hair. SIMIC produces a knife and, pulling WALKER's head back, cuts off a large part of WALKER's hair (her ponytail), this causes her to fall to the ground. Falling to the ground causes WALKER to drop the baby and consequently the baby is caused slight injury when it hits the pavement (some minor bruising to the baby's arm).

Thinking about the law relating to offences of assault (particularly the offences of assault contrary to s. 39 of the Criminal Justice Act 1988 and s. 47 of the Offences Against the Person Act 1861), which of the following comments is correct?

A SIMIC has committed a s. 39 offence against WALKER and also the 6-month-old baby (a battery in both cases).
B SIMIC has committed a s. 39 battery offence against WALKER but no offence in relation to the 6-month-old baby.
C SIMIC has committed a s. 47 assault against WALKER and a s. 39 offence (a battery) against the 6-month-old baby.
D SIMIC has committed a s. 47 assault against WALKER and the 6-month-old baby.

30. LOCKETT is in a pub when she is approached by FEARLY, who is drinking with a group of his friends. FEARLY tries to engage LOCKETT in conversation and asks if she would like a drink; LOCKETT is not interested in FEARLY and politely says *'No thanks'*. FEARLY's friends roar with laughter at his rejection and, feeling humiliated and for the purposes of his sexual gratification, FEARLY puts his hands on LOCKETT's breasts (over the top she is wearing) and shouts *'Well, how about a fuck then!'*

Would this constitute an offence of sexual touching (contrary to s. 3 of the Sexual Offences Act 2003)?

A Yes, because touching includes touching through the clothing.
B No, FEARLY did not touch LOCKETT's genitals.
C Yes, because FEARLY did it for the purposes of sexual gratification.
D No, because the touching was not with FEARLY's penis.

31. OLIVER works in the offices of a small factory as an administration clerk and one of the functions of his job is to pay weekly wages to the all the staff (which includes OLIVER); the wages are paid in cash). OLIVER is overworked and tired and on the day he pays wages he accidentally puts an extra £50 into his wage packet and the wage packet of BAINES (a factory worker). The wages are paid out and the factory staff leave for the weekend. When BAINES gets home, he opens his wages and realises there has been an error and he has been paid an extra £50. Thinking himself lucky, he decides (dishonestly) to keep the money. When OLIVER counts his wages that evening, he realises the error he has made but, feeling aggrieved because he is overworked, he decides to keep the money he accidentally paid into his own wage packet.

Considering the law in relation to the offence of theft (contrary to s. 1(1) of the Theft Act 1968), which of the following comments is correct?

A BAINES commits an offence of theft; OLIVER does not.
B The offence of theft has not been committed by either person.
C BAINES and OLIVER commit theft.
D OLIVER commits theft; BAINES does not.

32. KENNEDY travels all over England and Wales doing odd jobs for cash payments and travelling from place to place by hitching rides, usually in haulage vehicles that carry goods. He is contacted by DUDLEY who tells KENNEDY he has work for him in Newcastle and the job starts tomorrow. KENNEDY is 190 miles away in Stoke-on-Trent and tries to hitch a lift but is unsuccessful. Desperate to get to Newcastle, KENNEDY manages to force open the back door of a haulage vehicle at a motorway service station (KENNEDY overheard the driver stating that he was transporting goods to Newcastle) and waits in the back of the vehicle to travel to Newcastle. The driver returns to the vehicle and drives off. The vehicle has travelled 100 miles before the driver discovers KENNEDY in the rear of the vehicle.

Does KENNEDY commit an offence of obtaining services dishonestly (contrary to s. 11 of the Fraud Act 2006)?

A Yes, and as the offence is a 'conduct' crime; it is committed when KENNEDY gets into the haulage vehicle intending to travel to Newcastle.
B No, the offence requires a fraudulent act to be carried out—this has not occurred in this situation.
C Yes, and as the offence is a 'result' crime, the offence is committed once the vehicle drives off from the motorway service station.
D No, as KENNEDY is not obtaining a service (the haulage company does not provide rides to people).

33. LEDDY needs £20,000 to pay off a loan he took from CORBIN (a violent money-lender). LEDDY approaches COOPER and MARR for some assistance. COOPER suggests that LEDDY commits a burglary by stealing jewellery from a shop and selling it to raise the cash to pay off the debt. He tells LEDDY that he knows a good target shop and that he will assist him to commit the crime and act as a look-out for him when he breaks into the jewellery shop. MARR tells LEDDY that he knows how to disable the alarm systems protecting the shop and offers LEDDY instruction on how to accomplish that task. With the help of COOPER and MARR, LEDDY breaks into the jewellers and steals £50,000 of jewellery. However, the police attend the scene and, although LEDDY escapes, COOPER is arrested which leads to the arrest of MARR. Despite all the efforts of the police, LEDDY is never traced or identified.

Considering the law relating to principles and accessories, which of the following comments is correct?

A As the principal offender (LEDDY) cannot be traced or identified, COOPER and MARR cannot be tried as accessories to the offence.
B If found guilty as accessories to this offence (burglary), COOPER and MARR would be treated in the same way as if they were tried in a magistrates' court (a maximum term of imprisonment of six months for this offence).
C COOPER is an accessory to LEDDY's burglary as he was at the scene of the offence; MARR is not an accessory in these circumstances.
D COOPER and MARR are accessories to LEDDY's burglary. They can be tried and, if found guilty, will be treated in the same way the principal offender (LEDDY) would be for this indictable offence.

34. DURRANT is driving his car along a street when he sees RAWSON walking along the pavement. DURRANT thinks that RAWSON is dressed provocatively and believes she is a prostitute. DURRANT slows down as he passes RAWSON, lowers the front passenger-side window of his car and says *'I'll give you £50 for sex—is that enough?'* RAWSON is not a prostitute but is amused by DURRANT and says *'Say it to my face and who knows?'* DURRANT stops his car, gets out and approaches RAWSON and says *'I'll give you £50 for sex—what do you say?'* RAWSON laughs at DURRANT and says *'In your dreams, dickhead!'* and walks off. At no stage is RAWSON anything other than amused by DURRANT.

In relation to the offence of soliciting by 'kerb-crawling' (contrary to s. 51A of the Sexual Offences Act 2003), which of the following statements is correct?

A DURRANT does not commit the offence as RAWSON is not a prostitute.
B DURRANT commits the offence but only when he approaches RAWSON in the street.
C DURRANT does not commit the offence as he does not cause annoyance to RAWSON.
D DURRANT commits the offence when he asks RAWSON for sex when he is in his car.

35. RHODES works in a bar but his wages are not enough to support his lifestyle so he decides to commit offences of fraud and robbery to get extra cash. His plan is to serve customers at the bar and watch them. If they become drunk and then use credit or debit cards to pay for their drinks, he will 'clone' the card details and use the details to commit fraud offences. When they leave the bar, he will quickly follow them, attack them and steal from them. To commit the fraud offences, he brings a machine to clone the card details to his workplace; to commit the robbery offences, he brings a balaclava and some pepper spray. He stores all of the items in a small storeroom next to the bar, intending to carry out the offences later that evening if the opportunity arises.

In relation to the offence of going equipped (contrary to s. 25 of the Theft Act 1968), which of the following comments is correct?

A RHODES does not commit the offence as robbery and fraud are not offences associated with the offence of going equipped.
B RHODES does not commit the offence as he does not have the items with him in a public place.
C RHODES commits the offence but only in respect of the balaclava and the pepper spray to be used in robbery offences.
D RHODES commits the offence but only in respect of the machine to clone the card details.

36. John HAMILTON and Mark HAMILTON are civil partners who share a fantasy about raping STONE (their next-door neighbour). John wants to take this further and actually commit the offence and speaks to Mark about it. They agree that they will wait for STONE as she leaves her house the following morning, kidnap her and bring her back to their house where they will take turns raping her. The pair wait for STONE to leave her house the following morning but, unknown to either of the men, she has been involved in a car accident and is detained in an Accident and Emergency ward of a nearby hospital, meaning that their plan cannot be executed.

Considering only the offence of statutory conspiracy (contrary to s. 1 of the Criminal Law Act 1977), which of the following comments is correct?

A The offence is not committed as the men are civil partners.
B The offence is not committed as it is impossible to commit the offence.
C The offence is not committed as three people are required to commit a statutory conspiracy.
D The offence under s. 1 is not committed as the *mens rea* of this offence requires 'dishonesty'.

37. RICHARDSON is HIV-positive and is aware of that fact. One afternoon, RICHARDSON is speaking to FLETCHER (his neighbour) and she confesses that she has always wanted to have sex with him. She invites RICHARDSON into her house where she tells RICHARDSON that she wants to have sexual intercourse with him. RICHARDSON believes that if he uses a condom the risk of him passing the HIV virus to FLETCHER, although still possible, will be significantly reduced and on that basis he has protected sexual intercourse with FLETCHER (penis to vagina) using a condom. A few days later, FLETCHER is told by another neighbour that RICHARDSON is carrying the HIV virus. FLETCHER visits a police station and reports that she has been raped, stating that she would not have had sex with RICHARDSON had she known he was carrying the HIV virus. A later analysis of FLETCHER's blood reveals that she is HIV-positive (this can be traced back to her sexual activity with RICHARDSON).

Which of the following statements is correct in relation to RICHARDSON's liability?

A RICHARDSON would be guilty of recklessly causing FLETCHER grievous bodily harm (contrary to s. 20 of the Offences Against the Person Act 1861).

B RICHARDSON would be guilty of assault (contrary to s. 47 of the Offences Against the Person Act 1861).

C RICHARDSON commits rape (contrary to s. 1 of the Sexual Offences Act 2003) in these circumstances as he did not tell FLETCHER that he was HIV-positive.

D RICHARDSON would be guilty of rape (contrary to s. 1 of the Sexual Offences Act 2003) if he had not taken measures to protect FLETCHER by wearing a condom.

38. WHARTON visits a large agricultural show held in the private grounds of a country home—entry to the show and grounds is open to members of the public who pay a £5 entry fee. WHARTON is seen behaving in a suspicious manner near to several luxury cars on a display stand and the manager of the display is concerned and contacts the police who have posted several officers to the show. PCs LOW and BISHMAN visit the stand and as they get closer to it they see WHARTON walking towards them. They stop WHARTON and carry out a lawful search under s. 1 of the Police and Criminal Evidence Act 1984. During the course of the search, they search a bag WHARTON is carrying and inside that bag they find a single shot 'airsoft gun' (which has a kinetic energy level of 1.34 joules) and a telescopic sight for a rifle (not the airsoft gun in WHARTON's bag). WHARTON tells the officers that he does not possess a firearms certificate of any description.

Does WHARTON commit an offence of possession of a firearm in a public place (contrary to s. 19 of the Firearms Act 1968)?

A Yes, but only in relation to the airsoft gun.

B No, it is not an offence to possess an airsoft gun of this type (it is not a firearm), nor is it an offence to possess a telescopic sight for a rifle (it is not a firearm).

C Yes, but only in relation to the telescopic sight for the rifle.

D No, WHARTON is not in a public place.

39. Three months ago, KHAN committed an offence of handling stolen goods (contrary to s. 22 of the Theft Act 1968). Since then, he has been arrested and charged with the offence and at court he has pleaded 'not guilty' to the charge. KHAN has a conviction for theft which is four years old and another conviction for theft which is three years old.

Could KHAN's previous convictions be submitted as evidence of previous misconduct (under s. 27 of the Theft Act 1968)?

A No, as the previous convictions relate to theft rather than handling stolen goods.
B Yes, in relation to both previous convictions for theft.
C Yes, but only in respect of the previous conviction for theft which is three years old.
D No, the previous convictions can only be introduced if there is also evidence that KHAN was involved in an offence of handling stolen goods in the last 12 months.

40. WOOD owns a 'side-by-side' shotgun which he has been using frequently during the shooting season. WOOD believes the shotgun needs a minor repair to the barrel and is talking about this to LUCY while they are playing a round of golf. LUCY tells WOOD not to bother paying to have the shotgun repaired by an experienced gunsmith as he has been earning money for years by servicing and repairing shotguns (although he is not a registered firearms dealer and does not have a firearms certificate). LUCY tells WOOD that he will service and repair the shotgun for a fraction of the price (he offers to do this for £100). WOOD agrees and LUCY services and repairs the shotgun.

Would LUCY commit an offence under s. 3 of the Firearms Act 1968 (dealing with business and other transactions with firearms and ammunition)?

A Yes, because he charged WOOD for the service and repair (if it was carried out for free then no offence would be committed).
B No, the offence only applies to s. 1 firearms.
C Yes, because by way of trade or business he has repaired a shotgun without being registered as a firearms dealer.
D No, LUCY is not exposing a firearm for sale or transfer.

41. PICKERING is a paedophile with several convictions for sexual offences against children. He is concerned about being caught carrying out his crimes as he is sure he will be given an exceptionally long prison sentence if he is. To minimise the risk of conviction, he pays TAYLOR to obtain the sexual services of a child for him (PICKERING wants to be masturbated by the child), telling TAYLOR to make sure the child is 16 years old and that the child is aware that they will be well paid for their services. TAYLOR tells HAZEL (his 17-year-old nephew) about PICKERING and persuades HAZEL to pretend to be 16 and masturbate PICKERING. HAZEL agrees, meets PICKERING (who believes HAZEL is 16 years old) and masturbates him.

Does PICKERING commit an offence contrary to s. 47 of the Sexual Offences Act 2003 (paying for the sexual services of a child)?

A Yes, PICKERING commits the offence because he believes the activity is with a 16-year-old child.
B No, HAZEL is not a child under 16.
C Yes, because HAZEL is under 18 and PICKERING does not reasonably believe HAZEL is 18 or over.
D No, HAZEL did not have sexual intercourse with PICKERING.

42. DYSART (aged 22 years) has a keen interest in firearms and is considering purchasing a firearm that would be subject to the law (and associated rules and regulations) under s. 1 of the Firearms Act 1968. His uncle, OLNEY, possesses a s. 1 firearms certificate and, aware of DYSART's interest in firearms, gives DYSART a gift of several different types of ammunition which consists of a bullet for a rifle and a cartridge containing ten shot (none of which is bigger than 0.36 inches in diameter).

Would DYSART's possession of these two types of ammunition amount to an offence under s. 1 of the Firearms Act 1968 (possession etc. of a firearm or ammunition without a certificate)?

A No, as DYSART is over 21 years old.
B Yes, but only in respect of the bullet for the rifle.
C No, as he did not purchase the ammunition (it was given as a gift).
D Yes, the offence is committed in relation to both types of ammunition.

43. SCOTT approaches CANNING (who does not know SCOTT) and tells him that unless he kills DARROW immediately, his wife and child will be killed. SCOTT produces a gun and several photographs of CANNING's family and tells him that he has been observed for some time. SCOTT gives CANNING the gun and DARROW's details and, believing that SCOTT will kill his wife and child, CANNING goes to DARROW's house and kills him. CANNING is arrested at the scene and states that the only reason he committed the offence was because he was placed under duress.

Would CANNING be able to use this defence?

A No, as the defence is not available in respect of an offence of murder.
B Yes, as the threat drove CANNING to commit the offence.
C No, as the threat of harm must be made solely to the person who goes on to commit the relevant offence.
D Yes, as the offence was carried out immediately after the threat was made.

44. PLUCINSKI is the 'special guardian' of Gemma STAPLEY (who is 14 years old); they live together in Birmingham. Gemma has shown an interest in Polish history and PLUCINSKI asks her if she would like to visit his relatives in Warsaw and Lublin (large cities in Poland). Gemma states that she would love to do that so PLUCINSKI arranges an extended five-week visit for Gemma where she will stay for three weeks in Warsaw and two weeks in Lublin before returning home to Birmingham. PLUCINSKI mentions the trip to Gemma's mother (Jane STAPLEY) who, out of spite, states that she does not want her daughter to go on the trip. PLUCINSKI ignores Jane's comment and sends Gemma to Poland for five weeks.

Would PLUCINSKI commit an offence under s. 1 of the Child Abduction Act 1984 in this situation?

A No, as Gemma STAPLEY's special guardian, PLUCINSKI can take or send Gemma STAPLEY out of the United Kingdom for as long as he likes.
B Yes, the offence is committed the moment he sent Gemma STAPLEY out of the United Kingdom.
C No, as PLUCINSKI is Gemma STAPLEY's special guardian and has sent her out of the United Kingdom for a period of less than three months.
D Yes, the offence is committed once Gemma STAPLEY is out of the United Kingdom for one month or more.

45. HEWSON is a drug dealer and is involved in a dispute with GILCHRIST (a rival drug dealer). HEWSON decides to intimidate GILCHRIST by breaking into his house, leaving a pig's head in GILCHRIST's bed and spraying 'DIE PIG SCUM' in GILCHRIST's bedroom (committing criminal damage in the process). HEWSON watches GILCHRIST's house and when he leaves HEWSON breaks in. He is making his way upstairs when GILCHRIST's wife appears and, thinking this is an even better opportunity to intimidate GILCHRIST, HEWSON rapes GILCHRIST's wife. HEWSON then places the pig's head in GILCHRIST's bedroom, sprays the graffiti 'DIE PIG SCUM' on the bedroom wall and leaves.

Which of the statements below correctly identifies HEWSON's criminal liability in relation to the offence of burglary?

A A burglary under s. 9(1)(a) of the Theft Act 1968 is committed when HEWSON breaks in intending to cause criminal damage.
B A burglary under s. 9(1)(b) of the Theft Act 1968 is committed when HEWSON rapes GILCHRIST's wife.
C An aggravated burglary (under s. 10 of the Theft Act 1968) is committed when HEWSON rapes GILCHRIST's wife.
D A burglary under s. 9(1)(b) of the Theft Act 1968 is committed when HEWSON commits criminal damage in the bedroom.

46. LITTLE (aged 17 years) is on holiday and sitting on a bench on a seafront smoking cannabis. PC DERRY is walking behind the bench; he smells the cannabis and sees LITTLE smoking. PC DERRY approaches LITTLE and lawfully searches him under s. 23 of the Misuse of Drugs Act 1971. During the search, PC DERRY finds a small amount of cannabis in LITTLE's pocket and, as the officer finds the drug, LITTLE says, *'It's only a little bit—just for me on holiday.'* PC DERRY is satisfied that the cannabis he has found is only for personal use by LITTLE.

Could PC DERRY deal with LITTLE by way of a Penalty Notice for Disorder (PND) in respect of possession of the cannabis?

A No, as cannabis is a Class B drug and the scheme only relates to Class C drugs.
B Yes, such a PND could be issued to anyone who is 16 or over.
C No, PNDs are not appropriate for offenders under the age of 18.
D Yes, a PND can be used for possession of any drug as long as the drug is possessed for personal use.

47. LAURIE is in some discomfort from whiplash injuries received in a car crash several days ago. He visits his local surgery and speaks to Dr BROMWELL about the whiplash who states that the treatment he is receiving is ample to deal with the situation which will improve rapidly over the next week. LAURIE is adamant that he is suffering a lot of pain and demands that Dr BROMWELL give him an injection of morphine to lessen the pain. Dr BROMWELL tells LAURIE that such a treatment is out of the question. LAURIE honestly believes that he has a lawful right to the pain-killing injection and tells Dr BROMWELL that if he does not give him the injection, he will beat Dr BROMWELL up as soon as his whiplash injuries are gone in a week or so (LAURIE realises that assaulting Dr BROMWELL is an unlawful act in itself).

Considering the offence of blackmail (s. 21 of the Theft Act 1968) alone, which of the following comments is correct?

A As LAURIE honestly believes that he has a right in law to the injection, there is no 'dishonesty' involved in this situation and the offence is not committed.
B LAURIE has committed the offence of blackmail in these circumstances.
C Blackmail has not been committed as the menace LAURIE uses does not relate to something that will take place 'then and there'.
D This would not amount to blackmail as LAURIE is not seeking any kind of material profit.

48. FERGIE finds out that his girlfriend (JAMISON) is having an affair with his best friend (BROWN). FERGIE decides that he will get revenge on the pair by causing them really serious harm and plans to wait until they are having sex with each other and to burst in on them and throw strong acid over the pair. His intention is to cause them horrific burn injuries that will scar them for the rest of their lives. As FERGIE works in a laboratory, he has access to chemicals and obtains a container of hydrofluoric acid. He pretends to go to work and waits until he sees BROWN visit his house. He sneaks into the house and bursts into a bedroom where JAMISON and BROWN are having sexual intercourse and he shakes the acid container towards the pair. But as FERGIE was so emotional he forgot to take off the top of the container and no harm is caused to JAMISON or BROWN.

Does FERGIE commit an offence of attempted murder (contrary to s. 1 of the Criminal Attempts Act 1981) in this situation?

A No, as FERGIE does not intend to kill JAMISON and BROWN.
B No, it is impossible for the offence to be committed (the top has not been removed from the container).
C Yes, when he bursts into the bedroom.
D Yes, when he shakes the container towards JAMISON and BROWN.

49. MAHON has an argument with JACOB (her next-door neighbour) regarding noise from a party that JACOB is holding in his back garden. JACOB has positioned two large speakers in his back garden and MAHON says these are causing far too much noise. MAHON decides that she will cut the wires leading to the speakers that JACOB has set up in his garden and she has just the thing to accomplish that in her garden shed—telescopic pruning shears. She walks towards her shed to pick up the shears but as she does so a power surge blows JACOB's speakers and stops the noise.

Does MAHON commit an offence of possessing an article with intent to cause criminal damage (contrary to s. 3 of the Criminal Damage Act 1971)?

A Yes, when she decides to use the shears to cut the speaker wires.
B No, this activity is taking place in a private garden not a public place.
C Yes, but not until she begins to walk towards the garden shed.
D No, as she never picked up the shears, she never physically possessed them.

50. Hannah DUFFIELD has three daughters: Caroline (who is 17 years old), Georgina (who is 16 years old) and Lorraine (who is 5 years old). Hannah is going away for a week with some friends and tells Caroline that she is 'in charge' of the house while she is away and that she is to look after her two younger sisters. Caroline is very angry about this as she had her own plans that week but Hannah tells Caroline that she has no choice and she must do as she is told. During the week that Hannah is away, Caroline argues with Georgina and physically assaults her several times. Out of spite, Caroline deliberately does not feed Lorraine for the entire week causing Lorraine suffering as a result.

Does Caroline commit the offence of child cruelty (contrary to s. 1 of the Children and Young Persons Act 1933)?

A Yes, Caroline commits the offence against Georgina and Lorraine.
B Yes, Caroline commits the offence but only against Lorraine.
C No, Caroline does not commit the offence (she is under 18).
D No, Caroline does not commit the offence (she is not the parent of either child).

51. LAW is driving his daughter to school in a Bentley Continental GTC convertible car with the roof down; LAW's daughter is listening to loud music on a set of headphones. LAW has to stop at a set of traffic lights and whilst waiting he is approached by BAYLEY who is in a very sorry state as he is homeless, wearing filthy clothing and has not cleaned or shaved for several weeks. BAYLEY has a paper cup in his hand and asks LAW if he has any spare change to which LAW replies that he has not. BAYLEY looks at LAW and feels angry about the fact that LAW has so much and says *'Give me a tenner then—and, if you don't, I'll piss in your car, you rich bastard!'* LAW laughs at BAYLEY and tells him to *'Get lost'*, at which point BAYLEY says, *'Give me the money or I'll punch your kid in the face!'* LAW's daughter is oblivious to what is going on as she did not hear BAYLEY's threat but LAW believes BAYLEY and, fearing for the safety of his daughter, he hands £10 to BAYLEY.

Considering the offence of robbery (contrary to s. 8 of the Theft Act 1968), which of the following statements is correct?

A The offence of robbery is committed when BAYLEY threatens to damage LAW's car by urinating in it.
B The offence of robbery is committed when BAYLEY threatens LAW's daughter.
C The offence of robbery is committed when LAW hands over the £10 note.
D No offence of robbery has been committed in this situation.

52. ROWLAND and MEAD work in the same office and hate each other. They both apply for a promotion in the workplace which ROWLAND gets. MEAD is convinced that ROWLAND obtained the promotion by smearing his abilities to several members of the interview panel and when ROWLAND is standing not too far from MEAD in the office and boasting to another member of staff how he got the job 'with ease', MEAD snaps. Intending to make ROWLAND believe he is going to be killed MEAD shouts *'I'm fucking sick of you and tonight I'm going to come round to your house and blow your bloody head off!'* (MEAD does not actually intend to follow through with the threat). ROWLAND laughs at MEAD as he does not believe the threat at all and thinks MEAD is pathetic.

In respect of the offence of making a threat to kill (contrary to s. 16 of the Offences Against the Person Act 1861), which of the following comments is correct?

A MEAD has committed the offence in these circumstances.
B As MEAD does not intend to carry out the threat, the offence is not committed.
C As ROWLAND does not believe MEAD, the offence is not committed.
D As the threat is to kill in the future (rather than there and then), the offence is not committed.

53. EVANS is at a large rock concert which he and tens of thousands of others have paid to attend. One of the female singers at the concert performs her act wearing a very revealing outfit which EVANS finds sexually stimulating. EVANS leaves the main concert arena and goes into one of the single portable toilets on the concert site. In the privacy of the single toilet, he masturbates and ejaculates.

With regard to the offence of engaging in sexual activity in a public lavatory (contrary to s. 71 of the Sexual Offences Act 2003), which of the following statements is correct?

A EVANS has committed the offence in these circumstances.
B The offence has not been committed as this is not a 'public' lavatory.
C The offence has not been committed as EVANS cannot be seen by another member of the public.
D The offence has not been committed as EVANS did not engage in sexual activity with another person.

54. PORTER is driving a Ford Transit van along a road when he is stopped by PC HARDWARE. PC HARDWARE searches the van and finds 10 illegal immigrants in the rear of the vehicle. PC HARDWARE arrests PORTER on suspicion of committing an offence of human trafficking under s. 2 of the Modern Slavery Act 2015.

Could PC HARDWARE detain PORTER's vehicle (the Ford Transit van) using the power under s. 12 of the Modern Slavery Act 2015?

A Yes, if an officer of the rank of inspector or above authorises the detention of the vehicle.
B No, PORTER would have to be charged with the offence before such action could be taken.
C Yes, if he has reasonable grounds to believe that an order for the vehicle's forfeiture could be made under the Act.
D No, the power of detention only applies to ships and aircraft.

55. BLACK is a member of a gang and meets a number of other gang members at a pub to discuss a fight that has been arranged with a rival gang. BLACK has a sports bag in his possession in which he has placed several knives to cause injury to the rival gang members during the fight. The group talk about what they will do during the fight and a discussion takes place regarding what weapons will be used. EARL (another gang member) produces an empty washing-up bottle that he has filled with hydrochloric acid and says that it can be used to cause injury to rival gang members. The gang laugh at EARL's suggestion and tell him not to be stupid. EARL is annoyed at being made to look a fool and decides he will use the washing-up bottle during the fight and prove the other gang members wrong. He slips the washing-up bottle containing acid into BLACK's bag (without BLACK's knowledge). On his way to the fight, BLACK is stopped by the police and his bag is searched resulting in the washing-up bottle containing acid being discovered.

In relation to the washing up bottle containing acid, does BLACK commit an offence under s. 5 of the Firearms Act 1968 (possessing or purchasing prohibited weapons or ammunition)?

A No, he did not know it was there.
B No, it is not a prohibited weapon.
C Yes, this is a strict liability offence.
D Yes, if it can be proved he knew 'something' was in the bag.

56. BARKER moves into a house directly opposite one owned by KENT. BARKER holds a series of noisy parties over several weeks resulting in KENT complaining about the noise and the police visiting BARKER's house. BARKER decides that he will cause serious problems for KENT and burn his house down. To do so, he makes a petrol bomb (using petrol, a milk bottle and an old rag). He waits until KENT's house is empty and walks over to the house. Outside the house, he lights the petrol bomb and throws it at KENT's house. As he does this, the rag falls out of the petrol bomb and the bottle hits the house, failing to ignite.

At what stage, if at all, does BARKER attempt to commit an offence of arson (under s. 1 of the Criminal Attempts Act 1981)?

A When he makes the petrol bomb.
B When he walks over to KENT's house.
C When he throws the petrol bomb at the house.
D The offence is not committed because the petrol bomb did not ignite.

57. KINGSTON (a 27-year-old male) attends a wedding where he speaks to DUDLEY (who is a 16-year-old female and the daughter of a family friend). KINGSTON engages DUDLEY in a conversation about horses as he knows DUDLEY is keen to learn to ride and is interested in equestrian events. KINGSTON tells DUDLEY he can get her free tickets to a major equestrian event in London and asks for her mobile number to contact her; DUDLEY provides her number. KINGSTON actually intends to send sexual messages to DUDLEY and the next day he sends a text message to DUDLEY asking her if she would like to have sexual intercourse with him.

    Does KINGSTON commit an offence under s. 15A of the Sexual Offences Act 2003 (sexual communication with a child)?

    A No, KINGSTON only communicated once to DUDLEY—this offence requires sexual communication to take place on two or more occasions.
    B Yes, the offence is committed when KINGSTON obtains DUDLEY's mobile number with the intention to sexually communicate with her.
    C Yes, the offence is committed when KINGSTON send the text message to DUDLEY.
    D No, because DUDLEY is 16 years old.

58. STARR has found out that KIERNAN (his girlfriend) has been having an affair with his best friend. STARR and KIERNAN live together in rented accommodation and have been saving for a deposit for a house. Out of a desire for revenge, STARR grabs a large tin of paint and pours it over £2,000 in cash that they had hidden in a drawer in the bedroom of the house. STARR then takes a pair of scissors and cuts up three designer shirts that KIERNAN had given to him as a birthday present.

    Has STARR committed an offence of criminal damage (contrary to s. 1(1) of the Criminal Damage Act 1971) in this situation?

    A Yes, to the money and the shirts.
    B No, money is not 'property' for the purposes of the Criminal Damage Act 1971 and you cannot cause criminal damage to property that you own (the shirts).
    C Yes, to the money alone.
    D No, the money and the shirts belong to STARR.

59. BOWES has fallen out with his ex-wife regarding the custody arrangements for their 13-year-old daughter. BOWES wants to take his daughter on holiday to Portugal but his ex-wife has refused permission. BOWES is fuming with his ex-wife and waits for her and his daughter to leave the house they live in and approaches them. He produces an imitation firearm (a pistol) and points it towards his ex-wife telling her that he is taking his daughter away to Portugal—he takes his daughter away and they fly to Portugal (BOWES commits an offence of child abduction under s. 1 of the Child Abduction Act 1984 in the process). A week later, BOWES is arrested in connection with the offence.

In relation to the offence of possessing a firearm while committing or being arrested for a sch. 1 offence (contrary to s. 17(2) of the Firearms Act 1968), which of the following comments is correct?

A The offence has been committed although it will be necessary for BOWES to be subsequently convicted of the child abduction offence in order to convict him of it.
B The offence has not been committed as an offence of child abduction contrary to s. 1 of the Child Abduction Act 1984 is not a sch. 1 offence.
C The offence has been committed in these circumstances.
D The offence has not been committed as BOWES used an imitation firearm when committing the child abduction offence.

60. GOODIER hates his wife and wants her dead. He plans to have her killed by a 'contract killer' while she is on holiday in Las Vegas, Nevada (in the United States). GOODIER has told REDSHAW (an American criminal associate of GOODIER's) about his plan and REDSHAW tells GOODIER he will make enquiries about locating a contract killer in Las Vegas to kill GOODIER's wife. REDSHAW's enquiries locate BURTON who is put in touch with GOODIER. GOODIER is in London when he telephones BURTON (who is in Las Vegas). During the telephone conversation, GOODIER offers BURTON $50,000 to murder his wife while she is on holiday in Las Vegas in two weeks' time.

Does GOODIER commit an offence of encouraging another to murder (contrary to s. 4 of the Offences Against the Person Act 1861)?

A Yes, as long as BURTON is actually encouraged to commit the murder.
B No, as the murder would occur in the United States.
C Yes, it does not matter whether BURTON is encouraged to kill GOODIER's wife.
D No, as BURTON is not a British national.

61. BLAIR is lawfully arrested under s. 24A of the Police and Criminal Evidence Act 1984 by DeVERE (a civilian) for an offence of theft. PC CHU attends the scene of the arrest and takes BLAIR into custody. Having considered the circumstances of the offence, PC CHU is satisfied that releasing BLAIR on bail ('street bail') is necessary and proportionate.

Could BLAIR be released on 'street bail' (s. 30A of the Police and Criminal Evidence Act 1984) in these circumstances?

A No, because BLAIR was arrested by DeVERE and not a police officer.
B Yes, as long as a custody officer must authorise BLAIR's release on bail (having considered any representations made by BLAIR).
C No, as BLAIR has been arrested for an indictable offence he must be taken to a designated police station.
D Yes, although PC CHU could not attach conditions to any bail given to BLAIR.

62. RANKINE (aged 20 years) is accused of committing an offence of theft from his employer. PC DAVISON arranges for RANKINE to voluntarily attend a police station to be interviewed regarding the offence. RANKINE attends the police station accompanied by FINLEY (RANKINE's legal representative). The interview takes place and RANKINE leaves having been told by PC DAVISON that he may be required to attend court in relation to the theft. It is decided that RANKINE should be charged with the theft and appear at magistrates' court to answer the charge.

In relation to the service of a summons or requisition, which of the following comments is correct?

A These documents could be served by handing them in person to RANKINE or to FINLEY.
B As RANKINE was legally represented, they must be served on FINLEY (they could not be served on RANKINE).
C They must be handed personally to RANKINE or posted to him at an address where it is reasonably believed that RANKINE will receive them (they could not be served on FINLEY).
D The documents must be served physically (by handing them to RANKINE or FINLEY); they cannot be served by post.

63. CLARKSON has been arrested on suspicion of burglary and taken to a designated police station. CLARKSON is interviewed about the offence by PC TELLER and is represented in the interview by his solicitor (WIGGINS). The interview is recorded using a secure digital recording network device and at the conclusion of the interview CLARKSON is handed a notice explaining how the recording will be used, arrangements for access to it and his rights to access should he be charged or informed he will be prosecuted/if he is not charged or informed he will be prosecuted (as per the requirements of para. 4.12 of Code E of the PACE Codes of Practice). CLARKSON accepts the notice but refuses to acknowledge receipt of it.

What course of action, if any, should be taken in these circumstances?

A PC TELLER will state for the recording that a copy of the notice has been provided to CLARKSON and that he has refused to acknowledge receipt of it.
B The custody officer should be called into the interview room to witness the fact that the notice has been handed to CLARKSON.
C PC TELLER should make a note in his pocket book that CLARKSON refused to acknowledge receipt of the notice and inform the custody officer who will note the fact in CLARKSON's custody record.
D No action is required as CLARKSON has accepted the notice.

64. FLINT has been arrested for an offence of fraud by PC CONWAY. The officer takes FLINT to a designated police station and reports the facts of the arrest to the custody officer, PS MILLER. As soon as PC CONWAY finishes relating the circumstances of the arrest to PS MILLER, FLINT says, *'It wasn't my idea—you know that someone else was involved, don't you?'*

Which of the following statements is correct with regard to the action that PS MILLER should take in response to this comment by FLINT?

A PS MILLER may question FLINT in respect of the comment he made in response to PC CONWAY's account.
B PS MILLER should note (on the custody record) any comment FLINT makes in relation to PC CONWAY's account, but should not invite comment.
C PS MILLER need not make any note of the comment made by FLINT.
D PS MILLER should caution FLINT before asking any questions about the comment made in response to the circumstances of the arrest.

65. NELDER and SENIOR were arrested and charged with possession of a controlled drug with intent to supply (contrary to s. 5(3) of the Misuse of Drugs Act 1971). NELDER confesses to the offence during his interview at a police station and states that he was going to supply the drugs and SENIOR knew nothing about them. SENIOR replies 'no comment' to all questions. They are both charged with the offence; NELDER pleads 'guilty' and is dealt with by the court; SENIOR pleads 'not guilty' and his case goes to trial during which SENIOR's defence team seek to use NELDER's confession in SENIOR's defence.

Would NELDER's confession be admissible in SENIOR's trial?

A Yes, as NELDER would be considered a witness rather than a defendant.
B Yes, as this is a confession by a co-accused.
C No, as SENIOR is no longer charged in the same proceedings.
D No, this is a confession from NELDER not SENIOR.

66. Authority has been given for MAY (a 20-year-old who has been arrested and is in police detention for an offence of possession with intention to supply a Class A drug) to be subject to an intimate search (under s. 55(1) of the Police and Criminal Evidence Act 1984). The search will be to recover a Class A drug that MAY is believed to have concealed in his rectum.

Which of the following comments is correct in relation to the person who can carry out that search and the location of the search?

A The search can be carried out by a police officer at a police station.
B An intimate search of this type can only take place at a hospital.
C An intimate search of this type may take place at a surgery.
D The search can be carried out by a police officer at a hospital.

67. KHADKA (aged 16 years) is in custody at a designated police station after having been arrested for an offence of burglary (a recordable offence which is contrary to the Theft Act 1968). Non-intimate samples have not been obtained from KHADKA in the course of the investigation and DC CULLIMORE, the officer in the case, now proposes to obtain those samples. KHADKA refuses to consent to the non-intimate samples being taken from him.

Which of the statements below is correct in relation to the taking of non-intimate samples in such a situation?

A As KHADKA is a juvenile, non-intimate samples cannot be obtained from him in this situation.
B An officer of the rank of inspector or above must authorise the taking of a non-intimate sample from KHADKA.
C A non-intimate sample cannot be taken from a detainee unless they provide written consent to the sample being taken.
D A non-intimate sample can be taken from KHADKA by force as long as a record is made of the circumstances and those present at the time the sample is obtained.

68. BLOOMFIELD (who is 17 years old) is a witness to an offence of s. 18 wounding where the victim was stabbed with a knife. LONGRIGG is arrested and charged with the offence and pleads 'not guilty' to it and a date has been set for the trial at Crown Court. BLOOMFIELD contacts the officer in the case, PC McMILLAN (who is also a witness in the case), and asks about the procedure in relation to her giving witness evidence in the Crown Court.

Considering the law regarding special measures contained in the Youth Justice and Criminal Evidence Act 1999, which of the following comments is correct?

A BLOOMFIELD would be eligible for special measures only if she were in fear or distress about testifying.
B BLOOMFIELD is automatically eligible for a special measures direction; PC McMILLAN would not be eligible for a special measures direction.
C The primary rule is that all witnesses under the age of 18 must give their evidence via video interview and live link—a witness under the age of 18 is prohibited from testifying in the Crown Court.
D Regardless of the nature of the offence, BLOOMFIELD is eligible to give evidence by video interview and the use of live link, but if she wishes to do so, she can testify in the Crown Court.

69. COTTER (aged 16 years) has been arrested in connection with the theft of a valuable painting (worth over £1 million) that has just taken place from a stately home she was visiting with her school. CCTV shows COTTER running out of the home with the painting and passing it to someone inside a car which left the scene. COTTER has just arrived at a designated police station and the arresting officer, PC STRONG, wants to carry out an urgent interview with her without an appropriate adult being present. The officer states that any delay in interviewing COTTER would hinder the recovery of the painting and wants to prevent that serious loss of property.

Which of the following statements is correct in relation to such an interview?

A The interview cannot take place as a juvenile cannot be interviewed without an appropriate adult being present.
B An officer of superintendent rank or above may authorise the interview in these circumstances.
C The interview cannot take place purely to prevent a serious loss of property.
D An officer of inspector rank or above may authorise the interview in these circumstances.

70. PC EDMONSON is called to the scene of a burglary in progress at a warehouse. When the officer arrives at the scene, he makes his way to the rear of the premises and sees that a door has been forced to gain entry. At that moment, RIDDING bursts out of the doorway, pushes the officer over and runs away from the scene. PC EDMONSON recognises RIDDING immediately as he has had numerous dealings with him and passes on RIDDING's details and description over the radio. RIDDING gets away but is arrested two days later by DC PARKER in respect of a number of burglary offences (including the warehouse burglary). When interviewed regarding the warehouse burglary, RIDDING is not legally represented and remains silent in response to all questions. DC PARKER is considering giving RIDDING a 'special warning' under s. 37 of the Criminal Justice and Public Order Act 1994 regarding his refusal to answer questions about his presence at the warehouse.

Could DC PARKER give RIDDING such a 'special warning' in these circumstances?

A Yes, but the 'special warning' must be delivered by PC EDMONSON.
B Yes, and if RIDDING fails to answer he can be convicted solely on an inference drawn from his failure or refusal to respond.
C No, RIDDING was not arrested at the warehouse, he was arrested elsewhere.
D No, RIDDING is not legally represented so a 'special warning' is not appropriate.

71. BEACH has committed an offence of fraud and a warrant for his arrest has been issued by a justice of the peace. PC LEWIS is trying to locate BEACH to execute the warrant but is having difficulty doing so. PC LEWIS believes that BEACH's ex-employer (a local authority) has information which would enable the officer to track BEACH down and execute the warrant. It is suggested that a disclosure order could be obtained (under s. 125CA of the Magistrates' Courts Act 1980) to require the local authority to supply information about BEACH.

If such an order is made, what information about BEACH could be required from the local authority?

A His name, date of birth or national insurance number and his address (or any of his addresses).
B His address (or any of his addresses) and any vehicle details that may assist in establishing his location.
C Any financial details (bank accounts and credit arrangements) that could lead to establishing his whereabouts.
D Any driving licence or passport details that could assist in tracing him for the purpose of executing the warrant of arrest.

72. Barry and Andrew CHALKLEY are married (under the terms of the Marriage (Same Sex Couples) Act 2013). The two have a stormy relationship as Barry has a very jealous nature. After an evening out, Barry accuses Andrew of having an affair and the pair argue, leading to Barry committing a s. 39 battery (contrary to the Criminal Justice Act 1988) against Andrew. The police are called and Barry is arrested. PC ALLEN obtains a witness statement from Andrew; Barry is later charged with the offence.

Considering the terms of s. 80 of the Police and Criminal Evidence Act 1984 and the compellability of spouses and civil partners to give evidence, would Andrew CHALKLEY be compellable to give evidence for the prosecution against Barry CHALKLEY in proceedings at court?

A Yes, the terms of s. 80 of the Police and Criminal Evidence Act 1984 do not apply to a same-sex marriage.
B Yes, as the terms of s. 80 of the Police and Criminal Evidence Act 1984 exclude offences involving injury to the spouse or civil partner of the accused.
C No, the offence involves an assault on a civil partner.
D No, civil partners are not compellable to give evidence against each other unless the offence involves really serious injury or is a sexual offence.

73. PS MOSS is performing the role of custody officer and has authorised the detention of VALENTINE and MUNDI in relation to an offence of violent disorder; the authorisation was made at 10 pm. At that time, VALENTINE was very obviously intoxicated through drink and was examined by a health-care professional who stated that this was the case. MUNDI appeared fit and healthy. Both men were placed in cells to be interviewed at a later time.

Considering Code C in relation to the care and treatment of detained persons, which of the following statements is correct?

A VALENTINE should be visited and roused at least every hour; MUNDI should be visited at least every hour but there is no need to wake him if he is asleep.
B VALENTINE should be visited and roused at least every half hour; MUNDI should be visited at least every hour but there is no need to wake him if he is asleep.
C VALENTINE should be visited and roused at least every hour; MUNDI should be visited at least every two hours but there is no need to wake him if he is asleep.
D VALENTINE should be visited and roused at least every half hour; MUNDI should be visited at least every two hours but there is no need to wake him if he is asleep.

74. PATRASCU has been arrested in connection with a sexual assault on a child and taken to a designated police station. PATRASCU is placed in a cell while the officers in the case get ready to interview him. When it is time to interview PATRASCU, he refuses to leave his cell—he sits in the corner of the cell stating that he is not going to speak to anyone about the offence because he has nothing to say about what he says are false allegations made against him.

Could PATRASCU be interviewed in his cell?

A No, the police require a suspect's consent to interview them regarding an offence.
B Yes, if the custody officer considers, on reasonable grounds, that the interview should not be delayed, the custody officer has the discretion to direct that the interview be conducted in a cell.
C No, as such an interview would be considered 'oppressive' under s. 76(8) of the Police and Criminal Evidence Act 1984 and be excluded from future proceedings.
D Yes, if an officer of the rank of inspector or above reasonably believes it is expedient and in the interests of justice to proceed in this manner, the interview may be conducted in a cell.

75. XIA has been arrested for offences relating to fraud and has been bailed to appear at a magistrates' court with several bail conditions including the provision of a surety; XIA's surety is SNOOK. Once he is released, XIA tells SNOOK that he has no intention of surrendering to the custody of the court and is going to escape to China. SNOOK writes to the police telling them of XIA's plan and that he no longer wishes to be a surety. PC WINN is the officer in charge of the case and is told about the situation. PC WINN visits XIA's home address and arrests him under s. 7 of the Bail Act 1976 based on the information the police received in the letter sent by SNOOK.

In relation to s. 7 of the Bail Act 1976 (the liability to arrest for absconding or breaking bail conditions), which of the following comments is correct?

A PC WINN should not have arrested XIA as XIA has not failed to surrender to the custody of the court or broken any bail conditions.
B XIA should be charged with an offence of breaking his bail conditions (under s. 7 of the Act) and brought before a court within 24 hours of his arrest.
C XIA should be brought before a judge of the Crown Court as soon as practicable.
D XIA must be dealt with by a justice as soon as practicable and in any case within 24 hours of being arrested.

76. DIXON has been charged with an offence of kidnapping and has pleaded 'not guilty' to the charge. The trial is taking place and DC MADDOX (the officer in the case and one of the interviewing officers) is being questioned regarding the interview with DIXON. During questioning, it is established that the copy of the interview with DIXON, which was recorded via removable recording media, has been accidentally destroyed. The only copy of the interview that remains is the original master recording and this is now required for the trial.

Which of the following comments is correct in relation to Code E of the PACE Codes of Practice and the procedures associated with the breaking of the seal on a master recording when it is required for a criminal trial?

A As the officer in the case, DC MADDOX may break the seal on the master recording.
B The seal should be broken by an officer of the rank of inspector or above (who is not directly connected to the case).
C A police officer shall arrange for the seal of the master recording to be broken in the presence of a representative of the Crown Prosecution Service.
D The seal should be broken by an officer of the rank of superintendent or above (who is not directly connected to the case).

77. Alison BARN has suffered years of abuse at the hands of Rodney BARN (her husband). One evening, Rodney attacks Alison and is in the process of punching her about the body when Alison reacts in self-defence and picks up a knife and stabs and kills Rodney. MASON (a neighbour of the BARNs) had heard the noise of the attack and walks into the BARNs' house and sees Alison standing over the body of Rodney holding the knife in her hand. MASON asks Alison, *'Did you kill him?'* In response, Alison nods her head. PC SIDHU is the first police officer at the scene and walks into the living room of the house. On seeing the officer, Alison states *'He left me no choice—I was defending myself, officer!'*

Considering the law regarding confessions under s. 82 of the Police and Criminal Evidence Act 1984, which of the following comments is correct?

A Alison's response to the question posed by MASON would not be a confession as it was not made in words.
B Alison's response to the question posed by MASON would not be a confession; the statement made to PC SIDHU would be.
C Alison's response to the question posed by MASON and the statement made to PC SIDHU would both be confessions.
D Alison's response to the question posed by MASON would not be a confession as it was not made to a person in authority.

78. HURST lives in a house opposite a pub which is well known for drug-dealing activities. One evening, there is a shooting outside the pub and HURST decides that he has had enough and contacts DC MOORE, telling the officer that he is more than happy for the police to use his house to carry out surveillance of the pub and put a stop to the drug-dealing outside. The police decide they will carry out an operation targeting the drug-dealing outside the pub but, in doing so, they are also considering the issues that HURST would face if it became known that his house was being used to carry out observations.

In relation to the ruling in *R* v *Johnson* [1988] WLR 1377 and the minimum evidential requirements needed if disclosure is to be protected, which of the following comments is correct in relation to police activity prior to the observations taking place?

A DC MOORE should visit HURST and ascertain HURST's attitude to the use of his house for observations and the possible disclosure of this use which could lead to the identification of the premises and HURST.
B An officer of the rank of sergeant or above should visit HURST and ascertain HURST's attitude to the use of his house for observations and the possible disclosure of this use which could lead to the identification of the premises and HURST.
C An officer of the rank of inspector or above should visit HURST and ascertain HURST's attitude to the use of his house for observations and the possible disclosure of this use which could lead to the identification of the premises and HURST.
D An officer of the rank of chief inspector or above should visit HURST and ascertain HURST's attitude to the use of his house for observations and the possible disclosure of this use which could lead to the identification of the premises and HURST.

79. Thomas and David LOWE are fraternal twins and are of roughly similar appearance. The pair carry out an offence of robbery and are arrested in connection with it but both dispute the eye-witness identification evidence. The identification officer and the officer in charge of the case consult each other and because a video identification is not practicable, it is decided to offer Thomas and David LOWE an identification parade.

Considering the requirements of Annex B of Code D of the Codes of Practice and the identification parade procedure, could Thomas and David LOWE be paraded together?

A No, Thomas and David LOWE must take part in separate identification parades.
B Yes, Thomas and David LOWE may be paraded together with at least 12 other people.
C No, unless an officer of the rank of inspector or above certifies that it is expedient to do so.
D Yes, Thomas and David LOWE may be paraded together with at least 16 other people.

80. DC BADHAM is the disclosure officer in relation to a case of rape. The case is complex and the victim, MacDONALD, provided a draft version of her witness statement in which there were some content differences to the final version of the witness statement. DC BADHAM is preparing material for disclosure and is considering his obligations in relation to the Disclosure Code of Practice (particularly in respect of the retention of material).

In relation to that Code, which of the following comments is correct?

A The duty to retain material would apply to the draft version of the witness statement from MacDONALD.
B The duty to retain material would apply to any duplicate copy of MacDONALD's final witness statement.
C In deciding what material should be retained in the investigation, DC BADHAM is not required to consider force orders.
D The duty to retain material would not be relevant to communications between the police and forensic scientists for the purpose of criminal proceedings.

81. LUCAS has been arrested on suspicion of committing an offence under s. 30 of the Sexual Offences Act 2003 (sexual activity with a person with a mental disorder impeding choice); the touching involved penetration of the victim by LUCAS. LUCAS has been interviewed and charged with the offence and the issue of bail is being considered. The custody officer, PS FREER, is aware that LUCAS has a single previous conviction which was for an offence of assault by penetration (contrary to s. 2 of the Sexual Offences Act 2003).

Would the provisions of s. 25 of the Criminal Justice and Public Order Act 1994 (police bail restrictions) be applicable to LUCAS?

A No, LUCAS does not have a conviction for an offence under s. 30 of the Sexual Offences Act 2003.
B Yes, and bail shall be granted if PS FREER is of the opinion that there are exceptional circumstances which justify it.
C No, LUCAS has not been charged with an offence of murder, attempted murder or manslaughter.
D Yes, and as a consequence LUCAS cannot be granted bail in any circumstances.

82. MARSH is in police detention having been arrested for an offence of assault by penetration (contrary to s. 2 of the Sexual Offences Act 2003). A witness statement from the victim of the offence has been obtained which includes a description of the person responsible for the attack. The victim states that her attacker had a large scar on his left hip and the officer in the case, DC DAY, is considering whether MARSH could be examined to establish if he has such a scar (using the powers under s. 54A(1) of the Police and Criminal Evidence Act 1984).

In relation to such an examination, which of the comments below is correct?

A MARSH cannot be examined to establish if he has a scar on his hip as the purpose of s. 54A(1) is solely to establish the identity of the person concerned.
B MARSH can be examined to discover if he has the scar on his hip but such an examination cannot be carried out using force.
C If MARSH refuses, then an officer of the rank of inspector or above can orally authorise that MARSH be examined to establish if he has the scar on his hip.
D An inspector must give an authorisation for MARSH's hip to be examined regardless of whether MARSH provides his consent to the examination.

83. BAY is arrested in Glasgow (Scotland) at 22.20hrs on Tuesday evening on behalf of Hampshire Police who want to question BAY in relation to an offence of s. 18 wounding (Offences Against the Person Act 1861). DCs HUTTON and MICHEALS (Hampshire police officers) are sent to Scotland to pick up BAY and bring him back to Portsmouth police station. The officers arrive in Glasgow the day after BAY was arrested (Wednesday) at 09.00hrs. They transport BAY to Portsmouth crossing the border between England and Scotland at 10.30hrs that day. They stop in Birmingham at 14.00hrs that day to obtain refreshments (during this time BAY is lodged in a cell block in Birmingham city centre). They recommence their journey and enter the Hampshire police area at 16.30hrs and arrive at Portsmouth police station at 17.30hrs.

What would BAY's 'relevant time' be in this situation?

A 22.20hrs on Tuesday.
B 10.30hrs on Wednesday.
C 16.30hrs on Wednesday.
D 17.30hrs on Wednesday.

84. COXHEAD is in police custody at a designated police station having been arrested in connection with an offence of importing a controlled drug. COXHEAD was interviewed regarding the offence by DS BAIN (the officer in the case) and her colleague DC MURRAY. COXHEAD denied the offence and, in particular, disputes the evidence of several eye-witnesses. Due to the seriousness of the case, it is decided to hold an identification parade whilst COXHEAD is in police custody. However, there is difficulty locating an inspector to act as an 'identification officer' which is causing an unreasonable delay to the investigation.

In relation to such a situation, which of the following comments correctly sets out the procedure that should be followed?

A The explanation of the identification procedure and notice in relation to it could be provided to COXHEAD by the custody officer (who is not involved in the investigation).
B The explanation of the identification procedure and the notice in relation to it must be provided to COXHEAD by an officer of the rank of inspector or above who is not involved in the investigation.
C The explanation of the identification procedure and the notice in relation to it could be provided to COXHEAD by DS BAIN but not by DC MURRAY.
D The explanation of the identification procedure and notice in relation to it could be provided to COXHEAD by DS BAIN or DC MURRAY.

85. ALLSOPP (aged 18 years) has been arrested for an offence of burglary at a sports equipment warehouse. The police have a large amount of evidence that strongly implicates ALLSOPP in 25 other burglary offences which have all taken place in residential premises. DC GULL is the officer in charge of the case and he speaks to his supervisor, DS BEMBRIDGE, regarding ALLSOPP and the burglaries. DS BEMBRIDGE suggests that when ALLSOPP is charged with the burglary of the sports equipment warehouse, an application should be made to the magistrates' court to commit ALLSOPP to detention in a police station (under s. 128 of the Magistrates' Courts Act 1980) for the purpose of enquiring into offences.

In relation to such a procedure, which of the following comments is correct?

A If the application is granted, it will enable DC GULL to make enquiries into all of the burglary offences (including the burglary of the sports equipment warehouse).
B ALLSOPP can be committed to detention at a police station for a period not exceeding two clear days.
C ALLSOPP cannot be committed to detention as he is 18 years old (the power for a magistrates' court to commit a person to police detention only applies to a person who is over 21 years old).
D If ALLSOPP is committed to police detention, the conditions of his detention and periodic review will apply as if he were arrested without warrant on suspicion of having committed an offence.

86. JARVIS has been arrested on suspicion of possessing a controlled drug with intent to supply (contrary to s. 5(3) of the Misuse of Drugs Act 1971) and is in police detention. The controlled drug in question is cannabis resin (a Class B drug). The arresting officer, DC PLANGE, has informed the custody officer, PS SANCHEZ, that she saw JARVIS swallow something just prior to his arrest and believes this may be some of the controlled drug (cannabis resin). DC PLANGE suggests to PS SANCHEZ that it might be a good idea to carry out an X-ray or an ultrasound scan on JARVIS.

Considering the power under s. 55A of the Police and Criminal Evidence Act 1984 to take X-rays or ultrasound scans, which of the following statements is correct?

A An X-ray or ultrasound scan could be taken of JARVIS with the authorisation of the custody officer and the written consent of JARVIS.

B An X-ray or ultrasound scan could not be taken in this situation as cannabis resin is not a Class A drug.

C An X-ray or ultrasound scan could be taken of JARVIS with the written consent of an officer of the rank of inspector or above; force can be used to obtain the X-ray or ultrasound scan.

D An X-ray or ultrasound scan could not be taken in this situation as the power is available only when someone has swallowed something that might be used to harm themselves or another.

87. TAYLOR was arrested and interviewed regarding an offence of robbery. TAYLOR states that he is innocent and disputes the identification evidence of an eye-witness to the offence and, consequently, the police have arranged an identification parade. TAYLOR's solicitor, HUTT, has requested that he is present when the identification parade takes place.

In relation to the request by HUTT and the procedure dealing with video identification parades (in Annex A of Code D of the Codes of Practice), which of the comments below is correct?

A TAYLOR may be present when the video identification procedure takes place if he requests to be present and with the prior agreement of the identification officer.

B During the identification procedure HUTT would not be allowed to communicate with the eye-witness or the identification officer.

C If the identification officer is satisfied that HUTT's presence will not deter or distract the eye-witness from viewing the images and making an identification, then he can be present when the video identification procedure takes place.

D A supervised viewing of the recording of the video identification procedure by HUTT and/or TAYLOR may be arranged on request, at the discretion of the identification officer.

88. OAKLEY is 13 years old and is at a designated police station having been arrested for an offence of burglary. The officer in the case is DC WHITE who is considering taking footwear impressions from the shoes worn by OAKLEY as part of her investigation into the burglary offence (no footwear impressions have been taken in the course of the investigation).

In relation to such footwear impressions, which of the following statements is correct?

A Footwear impressions can only be obtained with the written consent of OAKLEY and an appropriate adult.
B Footwear impressions can be obtained but DC WHITE would require the consent of OAKLEY's appropriate adult.
C No consent is required as OAKLEY has been arrested in connection with a 'recordable' offence.
D Footwear impressions cannot be taken from OAKLEY as he is under the age of 14.

89. WEBSTER has been arrested for an offence of theft. He was taken to a designated police station where his detention was authorised by the custody officer (PS CHASE) at 08.56hrs. Inspector LEEDHAM carried out WEBSTER's first review at 14.00hrs that day.

Considering the issues dealt with by s. 40 of the Police and Criminal Evidence Act 1984 (dealing with reviews), which of the following comments is true?

A WEBSTER's second review shall not be later than six hours after the first review (20.00hrs).
B WEBSTER's second review shall not be later than nine hours after the first review (23.00hrs).
C WEBSTER's second review shall not be later than 12 hours after detention was first authorised (20.56hrs).
D WEBSTER's second review shall not be later than 15 hours after detention was first authorised (23.56hrs).

90. MAGUIRE has been arrested for an offence of attempted murder and is in custody at a designated police station. The custody officer, PS LEWIS, asks MAGUIRE if he wants anyone informed of his whereabouts and MAGUIRE responds by saying that he would like COATES to be told. The arresting officer, DC ROBERTSON, has information that suggests COATES was involved in the offence and objects to COATES being informed of MAGUIRE's whereabouts as it will alert COATES to the fact that he is wanted for the offence.

In relation to delaying MAGUIRE's right to have someone informed of his whereabouts, which of the following comments is correct?

A An officer of the rank of inspector or above can authorise the delay which cannot be delayed beyond 24 hours after the relevant time.
B An officer of the rank of superintendent or above can authorise the delay which cannot be delayed beyond 24 hours after the relevant time.
C An officer of the rank of inspector or above can authorise the delay which cannot be delayed beyond 36 hours after the relevant time.
D An officer of the rank of superintendent or above can authorise the delay which cannot be delayed beyond 36 hours after the relevant time.

91. FURBY has been charged with an offence of burglary and the custody officer, PS PROTHERO, is considering granting conditional bail to FURBY. One of the conditions that PS PROTHERO is considering is that FURBY provides a surety in order that he surrenders to custody in the future.

In relation to the provision of a surety under s. 8 of the Bail Act 1976, which of the following comments is correct?

A PS PROTHERO can impose the condition that FURBY will provide one surety—requiring FURBY to provide more than one surety is not permitted under the provisions of the Bail Act 1976.
B If a surety is identified and FURBY is granted bail but fails to surrender to custody, it will be necessary to prove that the surety had some involvement with FURBY's non-appearance in order for the cash or security involved to be forfeited.
C The imposition of a surety condition would require the authority of an officer of the rank of at least inspector.
D In considering the suitability of any proposed surety for FURBY, PS PROTHERO may have regard to the proximity of the surety to FURBY (i.e. the place of residence of the surety).

92. TOMKINSON has been arrested for a series of high-profile murders and taken to a designated police station to be questioned regarding the offences. Due to the complex and detailed nature of the offences alleged to have been committed by TOMKINSON, the interview team responsible for questioning him are considering how long they will have to deal with him and discuss a superintendent's custody time extension and also warrants of further detention from a magistrates' court.

Using all of those extensions, what is the maximum period that TOMKINSON can be kept in custody without being charged?

A 60 hours.
B 72 hours.
C 84 hours.
D 96 hours.

93. KING is unhappy about plans to build a prison near his home; he is particularly dissatisfied about the approach taken by Councillor BANNER who is supporting the planning application. KING knows BANNER lives in a house in a quiet residential street and stands outside BANNER's house at 09.00hrs holding a banner stating 'NO NEW PRISON HERE!' KING has a loudspeaker which he has turned up to full volume and is using to amplify his voice when he repeatedly shouts *'No new prison here!'* Several residents have complained about the noise and its impact, in particular the significant distress it is causing to them. PC COSTELLO (on uniform patrol) attends the scene and speaks to KING who says that he has every right to protest in this manner.

Considering the powers to deal with protests under the Public Order Act 1986, which of the following comments is correct?

A PC COSTELLO would have to call a supervisor to the scene (who must be an officer of the rank of inspector or above) to impose conditions on KING's protest.
B The Public Order Act 1986 does not provide powers to deal with 'one-person' protests and the officer would have to deal with the situation by using powers in other legislation.
C If PC COSTELLO reasonably believes that the protest will result in serious public disorder or serious damage to property, then he may impose conditions on the protest.
D PC COSTELLO may give directions imposing on KING such conditions as appear to be necessary to prevent the impact on local residents.

94. KEYSE injures himself while carrying out some DIY at home and he visits the Accident and Emergency ward of his local hospital for treatment. His injuries are described as 'minor' by hospital staff and he is treated and discharged. He visits a nearby pub and starts drinking and becomes angry at what he thinks is the dismissive way he has been treated and, four hours after being discharged, he returns to the Accident and Emergency ward where he is verbally abusive towards RUDD (a nurse on the ward) and also to ORCHARD (a member of the public receiving treatment on the ward). RUDD tells KEYSE to leave the ward; KEYSE refuses to do so.

Would KEYSE's behaviour amount to an offence under s. 119 of the Criminal Justice and Immigration Act 2008 (causing a nuisance or disturbance on NHS premises)?

A No, he is not a patient at the hospital.
B Yes, but only in relation to his behaviour towards RUDD.
C No, because he has been a patient at the hospital in the last eight hours.
D Yes, in relation to his behaviour towards RUDD and towards ORCHARD.

95. PC GORDON is speaking to her supervisor, PS CRACKNELL, about the Police (Conduct) Regulations 2020 and the Standards of Professional Behaviour. PC GORDON asks PS CRACKNELL what sanctions can be imposed on a police officer at a misconduct meeting if the conduct of the officer is found to amount to misconduct.

Which of the following would be a correct response?

A The lowest misconduct sanction available at a misconduct meeting is management advice.
B The sanctions imposed at a management meeting will be either a written warning or a final written warning.
C A sanction that could be imposed at a management meeting is a fine.
D The most severe sanction that could be imposed at a management meeting is a reduction in rank.

96. PC SADDINGTON is on uniform patrol when she is directed to a report of people riding pedal cycles in a dangerous way on a road outside a school. PC SADDINGTON attends the scene and on arrival sees RAMSDALE performing a 'wheelie' manoeuvre on a mountain bike on a road outside the school. PC SADDINGTON approaches RAMSDALE and requires him to stop, using her power under s. 163 of the Road Traffic Act 1988.

Is the officer acting in a lawful manner when using the power under s. 163 of the Road Traffic Act 1988 to stop RAMSDALE?

A Yes, the power under s. 163 can be used to stop a mechanically propelled vehicle or a cycle on a road.
B No, the power under s. 163 can only be used to stop a motor vehicle being driven on a road or public place.
C Yes, the power under s. 163 can be used to stop a motor vehicle or a cycle on a road or public place.
D No, the power under s. 163 can only be used to stop a mechanically propelled vehicle on a road.

97. JUBB and KATO are Manchester City fans and both are watching Manchester City playing Manchester United in a Premier League match (a designated football match). Twenty minutes before the match begins, a Manchester United player is warming up by running up and down the side of the pitch and, as he runs past the pair, JUBB shouts out an abusive racist insult to the player (based on his nationality). KATO thinks this is hilarious and repeats the insult immediately. The player is extremely insulted and reports the behaviour to a police officer who is posted to the player's tunnel in the ground.

Has an offence under s. 3 of the Football (Offences) Act 1991 (indecent or racialist chanting) been committed in these circumstances?

A No, the chanting did not take place during a 'designated football match'.
B No, as the chanting was not repeated by a group of three or more people.
C Yes, when JUBB initially shouts out the racialist insult.
D Yes, when KATO repeats the racialist insult.

98. Using her powers under s. 1 of the Police and Criminal Evidence Act 1984, PC BECKFORD (who is on uniform foot patrol) stops and searches a Ford Focus motor vehicle which is being driven by SAMUEL; SAMUEL is the only person in the vehicle. PC BECKFORD searches SAMUEL and the vehicle for the same object and using the same grounds (searching for stolen property) but does not find anything. Enquiries in relation to the vehicle reveal that MARSTON is the owner of the vehicle. PC BECKFORD makes a written record of the search on the spot using a single search record to record the search of SAMUEL and the vehicle. She provides a copy of the record to SAMUEL.

Has PC BECKFORD complied with the requirements created by the Police and Criminal Evidence Act 1984 and Code A of the Codes of Practice?

A Yes, and as a search record was provided to SAMUEL (the person in charge of the vehicle), MARSTON would have no entitlement to a copy of the search record.
B No, a separate record should have been made for each search (the search of SAMUEL and the search of the vehicle).
C Yes, but if MARSTON asks for a copy of the record of search then he is entitled to one if he makes the request within three months beginning on the date the vehicle was searched.
D No, where the owner of the vehicle searched is not present, the officer carrying out the search should leave a notice in the vehicle stating that it has been searched.

99. WARD is a supervisor of a team of 20 office employees. He becomes involved in a confrontation with another member of staff, resulting in WARD punching the other member of staff in the back of the head—this is reported to the police and an investigation into the offence commences. AGNEW witnessed the incident and WARD believes AGNEW is a potential witness in any proceedings against him for the offence. WARD is concerned about possible criminal charges and approaches AGNEW. Intending to intimidate AGNEW, he tells AGNEW that if he says anything about what he has seen then he will get a terrible staff report and miss his wages bonus. AGNEW tells WARD that he is not interested and if the police ask him, he will tell them what he saw. WARD takes a different approach and tells AGNEW not to say anything otherwise he will be assaulted; AGNEW is sure he can deal with WARD and is not intimidated at all.

Does WARD commit the offence of intimidating witnesses and jurors (contrary to s. 51 of the Criminal Justice and Public Order Act 1994)?

A No, as AGNEW is not actually a witness or a juror.
B Yes, the offence is committed when WARD tells AGNEW that he will get a poor staff report which will affect his wages.
C No, as AGNEW is not intimidated by the actions of WARD.
D Yes, the offence is committed but only when WARD threatens AGNEW with violence.

100. At 03.00hrs, a burglary in progress is reported to the police; the burglary is taking place at a small factory unit. The police arrive quickly and at the scene they detain and arrest BARON for the burglary although a second unidentified offender managed to escape from the scene. The police establish that BARON occupies a house that is a very short distance from the factory unit (40 yards away) and, because the police believe that the second offender may dispose of evidence relating to the burglary, they propose to search BARON's house as it is necessary to do so for the effective investigation of the burglary offence.

Which of the following statements is correct when considering the powers to search premises under the Police and Criminal Evidence Act 1984?

A The officers can search BARON's home address using the power under s. 18 of the Act but would require an authorisation from an officer of the rank of inspector or above before doing so.
B BARON's home address could not be searched using the power under s. 18 of the Act as BARON is not in 'police detention'.
C The officers can search BARON's home address using the power under s. 18 of the Act; the officers shall inform an officer of the rank of inspector or above of the search as soon as practicable after it is made.
D BARON's home address could not be searched under s. 18 without the written authorisation of an officer of the rank of inspector or above.

101. AUSTIN is employed by his local council as a maintenance manager. He has responsibility for a number of council employees who visit council houses and carry out maintenance and repairs to the premises. AUSTIN tells several of his workers to visit a council house occupied by BURN and carry out extensive refurbishment there. The house is not owned by the council, it is BURN's private property and BURN is AUSTIN's girlfriend. One of the council workers is suspicious about the job and, after the work has been carried out, he reports the matter to the police by speaking to PC KROHN. PC KROHN notes down some basic details on a piece of paper and tells the council worker that he will look into the matter. PC KROHN places the paper in his coat pocket and fully intends to investigate the matter but because he is so busy at work he accidentally forgets about the incident and no investigation takes place.

Considering the offence of misconduct in a public office (contrary to common law), which of the following statements is true?

A The offence has not been committed as AUSTIN is not a police officer and PC KROHN's lack of action was purely accidental.
B PC KROHN has committed the offence (his omission makes him liable) but AUSTIN has not committed the offence.
C AUSTIN and PC KROHN have committed the offence in these circumstances.
D Only AUSTIN has committed the offence in these circumstances.

102. McNAMARA is driving his Toyota Yaris motor vehicle on a road having just visited his local pub where he had drunk one pint of lager (McNAMARA is below the prescribed limit as a result and his ability to drive is not impaired). While he is driving, McNAMARA selects and lights a cigarette and is avoidably distracted by the action, causing him to crash into the back of a Ford Focus. ORUM is in the rear seat of the Ford Focus and is eight months pregnant. ORUM is taken to hospital and prematurely gives birth; however, the child dies as a result of injuries it received due to the accident occurring (the child died six hours after the accident occurred). The police attend the scene of the accident and PC DENNY asks McNAMARA to cooperate with a screening test under s. 6 of the Road Traffic Act 1988 which McNAMARA refuses saying he is not drunk. McNAMARA is arrested and taken to a police station. One hour after being arrested, McNAMARA is required to provide an evidential specimen of his breath for analysis under s. 7 of the Road Traffic Act 1988 and, again, McNAMARA refuses as he says he is not drunk.

Would this amount to an offence of causing death by careless driving when under the influence of drink or drugs (contrary to s. 3A of the Road Traffic Act 1988)?

A Yes, the offence is committed when McNAMARA fails to comply with the requirement to take a screening test in pursuance of s. 6 of the Road Traffic Act.
B No, McNAMARA is not actually unfit to drive through drink or drugs.
C Yes, the offence is committed when McNAMARA fails to provide an evidential specimen in pursuance of s. 7 of the Road Traffic Act 1988.
D No, McNAMARA has not caused the death of 'another'.

103. PCs COLE and ERSKINE (both male officers) are on uniform mobile patrol when they are directed to an address where two men have been seen acting suspiciously in the garden of a dwelling house. When the officers arrive at the address, they see DOVE standing in the front garden of the dwelling house and standing inside the hallway of the dwelling house they see JANMAN. The officers reasonably suspect that DOVE and JANMAN may have stolen articles on their person and wish to use their powers under s. 1 of the Police and Criminal Evidence Act 1984 to search both men.

Thinking about the issues in respect of s. 1 of the Police and Criminal Evidence Act 1984 and Code A of the Codes of Practice, can the officers search DOVE and/or JANMAN?

A Yes, if they reasonably believe DOVE does not reside in the dwelling and is there without the express or implied permission of someone who resides in the dwelling; they cannot search JANMAN.
B No, as search powers under s. 1 of the Police and Criminal Evidence Act 1984 cannot be exercised in a garden used as part of a dwelling or in any dwelling house.
C Yes, they could search both men if they reasonably suspect that they do not live in the dwelling house.
D No, not unless the officers reasonably believe that DOVE and JANMAN do not reside in the dwelling and that they are in the dwelling or on land used with it without the permission of the owner of the premises.

104. BOLTON owns a field and has called the police because he is having problems with trespassers. GREEN, PEARMAN and COOPER drove onto the land in a 4 × 4 vehicle towing a caravan and have been camped on the site for two days. When BOLTON discovered their presence, he told them to leave. In response, all three shouted abusive words to BOLTON and GREEN told BOLTON to *'Fuck off or I'll kick your head in'* causing distress to BOLTON in the process.

Could a direction to leave the land under s. 61 of the Criminal Justice and Public Order Act 1994 be given to GREEN, PEARMAN and COOPER?

A Yes, but only to GREEN as he was the only person to threaten the occupier (BOLTON) with violence.
B No, they do not have six or more vehicles between them.
C Yes, as they have caused distress and used threatening, abusive or insulting words or behaviour towards the occupier (BOLTON) of the land.
D No, the direction can only be given to a group of five or more people trespassing on land with the common purpose of residing on the land.

105. James COLLARD (aged 19 years) and Amy COLLARD (aged 21 years) are brother and sister and live in the same house with their mother and father. James COLLARD does not have a job and has little money, which is a problem for him as he is addicted to cannabis. Amy COLLARD works at a farm shop and is paid in cash every Friday. Throughout their lives together, James COLLARD has always been the dominant sibling although there has never been any violence between the pair. One Friday, Amy COLLARD returns from work having been paid and James COLLARD, requiring money to buy cannabis, approaches her and takes her handbag off her, saying *'I'm your brother and I'll be looking after your finances from this point on.'* He takes out her purse and removes her £200 wages returning £40 to her.

Considering the definitions of 'domestic abuse' and 'personally connected' (which are relevant to the Domestic Abuse Act 2021), which of the following comments is correct?

A James COLLARD and Amy COLLARD are 'personally connected' as they live in the same house.
B James COLLARD and Amy COLLARD are 'personally connected' as they are relatives.
C This is not 'domestic abuse' because the behaviour does not consist of a 'course of conduct'.
D This is not 'domestic abuse' as the act does not amount to physical or sexual abuse.

106. DC FISHLOCK (who is dressed in plain clothes) is driving an unmarked police vehicle along a road. Suddenly, a Fiat 500 motor vehicle being driven in front of DC FISHLOCK swerves and collides with a lamp post at the side of the road, damaging the Fiat 500 and the lamp post in the process. The officer stops, gets out of his vehicle, identifies himself as a police officer and speaks to BRADLEY who is the driver and only occupant of the Fiat 500 motor vehicle. Fortunately, BRADLEY is not injured. BRADLEY tells the officer that a dog ran out in front of his vehicle causing him to take avoiding action. Other than being slightly shaken up, BRADLEY appears to be fine and the officer does not suspect that he is under the influence of drink or drugs.

Can DC FISHLOCK require BRADLEY to take part in a preliminary test (under s. 6 of the Road Traffic Act 1988)?

A No, as the officer is not in uniform.
B Yes, and in addition DC FISHLOCK could administer the test.
C No, because the officer does not suspect that a person has been injured as a consequence of the accident.
D Yes, but the officer could not administer the test.

107. PC DAVIS is taking a witness statement from MOTTRAM (the security supervisor at a large retail store) regarding a burglary that occurred several days ago. The officer is with MOTTRAM in her office which has a bank of 16 screens in it showing a live feed from security cameras in the retail store. While PC DAVIS is taking the statement, MOTTRAM points out that the behaviour of FARR (a customer in the store who can be seen on one of the screens) seems odd. PC DAVIS and MOTTRAM watch FARR who is behaving is a very strange way, so much so that PC DAVIS forms the suspicion that FARR is about to commit an offence of theft from the store.

Considering powers of arrest under s. 24 of the Police and Criminal Evidence Act 1984, which of the following statements is correct?

A PC DAVIS cannot arrest FARR unless the officer reasonably believes an offence has been committed and FARR is guilty of it.
B PC DAVIS cannot arrest FARR in anticipation that an offence may be about to be committed.
C PC DAVIS can arrest FARR if he has reasonable grounds for suspecting that FARR is about to commit an offence.
D PC DAVIS can arrest FARR but only if the officer reasonably believes that FARR is about to commit an offence.

108. CORK has been involved in an accident whilst driving his Nissan X-Trail motor vehicle along a road. The only person who was injured in the accident was CORK and the only damage caused was to CORK's Nissan X-Trail. CORK was taken to hospital and is in an Accident and Emergency ward, as a patient at the hospital, receiving treatment for his injuries which are, as it turns out, relatively minor. PC ASKEW attends the hospital intending to ask CORK to take part in a preliminary breath test under s. 6(5) of the Road Traffic Act 1988.

Can PC ASKEW require CORK to cooperate with a preliminary breath test in this situation?

A No, not unless the medical practitioner in immediate charge of CORK's case has been notified of the proposal to make the requirement and does not object to the requirement being carried out.
B Yes, as long as PC ASKEW is in uniform.
C No, as the only person injured was CORK and the only vehicle damaged was CORK's vehicle, this is not an 'accident'.
D Yes, and if CORK fails the test he can be arrested under s. 6D of the Road Traffic Act 1988.

109. FOGARTY attends a police station at the request of PC MARRI. PC MARRI believes FOGARTY to be a witness to an offence of theft and wishes to ask FOGARTY some questions about the offence. FOGARTY arrives at the police station and, as soon as PC MARRI begins to speak to him, he tells the officer that he is not a witness and that he actually committed the offence of theft. PC MARRI considers it is necessary to arrest FOGARTY and does so.

Could FOGARTY be searched using the powers under s. 32 of the Police and Criminal Evidence Act 1984?

A Yes, but only for anything which FOGARTY might use to assist him to escape from lawful custody.
B No, as s. 32 is a power to search premises where the arrested person has been prior to arrest and not a power to search the arrested person.
C Yes, but only for anything which might be evidence relating to an offence.
D No, as FOGARTY has been arrested at a police station.

110. GIROLANI finds out that IVEY (his neighbour) has applied for planning permission to build an extension to his house. He sees a van belonging to 'WBI Construction Ltd' parked outside IVEY's house and establishes that the company had been contacted by IVEY to provide a quote for the cost of building the extension. GIROLANI sends a threatening letter to IVEY and also to WBI Construction Ltd stating that any activities associated with the extension should stop. The letters do not contain any threats of violence but are unpleasant and GIROLANI intends them to cause distress. When IVEY receives the letter, he is distressed and contacts the police and PC JAKEMAN is sent to investigate the incident.

Would GIROLANI's behaviour amount to an offence of harassment (contrary to ss. 1 and 2 of the Protection from Harassment Act 1997)?

A No, as 'harassment' requires the person to be caused alarm and distress rather than just 'distress'.
B No, as the letters do not threaten violence.
C No, GIROLANI's behaviour would not amount to a 'course of conduct'.
D No, as 'conduct' requires speech (the offence cannot be committed by sending a letter).

111. PC WHITLEY (an officer with five years' police service) has attended a first stage meeting regarding her unsatisfactory performance. Her supervisor, PS KEARNEY (PC WHITLEY's line manager), has listened to PC WHITLEY's representations in the meeting but considers that PC WHITLEY's performance is unsatisfactory. Consequently, a written improvement notice is sent to PC WHITLEY setting out the relevant performance issue and the improvement required. The notice also includes the relevant 'specified period' within which improvement is expected to be made.

Which one of the following comments is correct in relation to that 'specified period'?

A It is expected that the specified period for improvement would not normally exceed one month.
B A specified period set out after a first stage meeting can only be extended at a second stage meeting.
C It is expected that the specified period for improvement would not normally exceed three months.
D If a specified period is extended, the extension should not lead to the improvement period exceeding six months.

112. PC BUNN is on uniform patrol and is sent to a report of children drinking alcohol in a public park. When the officer arrives in the park, she can see EVERITT (aged 15 years) and LEWIS (aged 16 years) sitting on a park bench drinking from cans labelled as cider. PC BUNN speaks to EVERITT and LEWIS, establishes their ages and that they are drinking alcohol (the cans of cider). EVERITT has an unopened can of cider with her as well as the opened one she is drinking from. PC BUNN requires EVERITT and LEWIS to surrender the opened cans of cider and EVERITT to surrender the unopened can of cider. PC BUNN pours the cider from all of the cans down a drain and throws the empty cans in a bin.

In relation to the powers provided by s. 1 of the Confiscation of Alcohol (Young Persons) Act 1997, which of the following comments is correct?

A PC BUNN can remove EVERITT and LEWIS to their place of residence.
B The officer did not have a power to require the surrender of the unopened can of cider from EVERITT.
C PC BUNN can remove EVERITT to a place of safety and, if necessary, this could be a police station.
D The officer did not have the power to pour the cider down a drain.

113. LENNARD works in a factory and has developed feelings for PORTER (a co-worker at the factory) although LENNARD has said nothing of those feelings to PORTER. After they finish their shift at the factory, LENNARD follows PORTER to his house to find out where he lives. Two days later, LENNARD parks his car a short distance from PORTER's house and spies on PORTER. PORTER saw LENNARD following him home and was alarmed by LENNARD's behaviour but thought nothing more of it; now he sees LENNARD spying on him, he is concerned and becomes distressed by LENNARD's behaviour and calls the police.

Would LENNARD's activities amount to an offence of stalking (contrary to s. 2A of the Protection from Harassment Act 1997)?

A No, as LENNARD has not used or threatened violence at any stage.
B Yes, the offence is committed at the point when LENNARD follows PORTER home.
C No, as LENNARD's activities do not cause PORTER to fear that violence will be used against him.
D Yes, the offence is committed when LENNARD spies on PORTER.

114. GREGSON commits an offence of aggravated trespass (contrary to s. 68 of the Criminal Justice and Public Order Act 1994) by trespassing on land where a housing estate is being built and obstructing workers on the site (it was GREGSON's intention to obstruct the workers because he does not think the housing estate should be built). The police are called to the scene and PC SOUTHERN (on uniform mobile patrol) arrives to deal with the situation.

Can PC SOUTHERN give GREGSON a direction to leave the building site using the power under s. 69 of the Criminal Justice and Public Order Act 1994?

A Yes, because PC SOUTHERN is the 'senior officer present at the scene'.
B No, this has to be given by an officer of the rank of superintendent or above.
C Yes, because PC SOUTHERN is in uniform.
D No, this has to be given by an officer of the rank of inspector or above.

115. Due to significant and continuing problems with children and young people truanting from school and being involved in anti-social behaviour, a local authority has decided to authorise the powers available under s. 16 of the Crime and Disorder Act 1998 and has 'designated premises' within its area as a place to which children and young people of compulsory school age may be removed to.

In relation to the law under s. 16 of the Act (dealing with the removal of truants and excluded pupils to designated premises), which of the following comments is correct?

A The police officer directing that the powers available under the Act shall be available will be an officer of the rank of superintendent or above.
B A constable must have reasonable cause to suspect that a child is a truant or is an excluded pupil in order to use the powers that the Act provides.
C A constable using the power to remove a child or young person to 'designated premises' must be in uniform.
D The power is available if the child or young person is found in a private or public place.

116. LLEWELLYN and JESSOP dislike each other intensely and have had a number of arguments about rugby (they play for opposing teams). The pair are at a private party at a house owned by BROWN and are both in the kitchen of the house when LLEWELLYN sees JESSOP and, intending JESSOP to believe that violence will be used against him, says *'Watch out next week when we play, I'll be looking to do you some harm.'* JESSOP does not believe LLEWELLYN and laughs at him, replying *'You're such a dick, aren't you?'* LLEWELLYN loses his temper and says *'That's it, I'll do you right now you bastard!'* JESSOP continues to laugh at LLEWELLYN, never worried that he will actually do anything as he believes LLEWELLYN is making empty threats.

At what point, if at all, does LLEWELLYN first commit the offence of fear or provocation of violence (contrary to s. 4 of the Public Order Act 1986)?

A When LLEWELLYN threatens to use violence against JESSOP the following week.
B The offence is not committed as the incident takes place in a dwelling and both individuals are in that dwelling.
C When LLEWELLYN threatens to use violence on JESSOP 'right now'.
D The offence is not committed as an offence under s. 4 of the Act can only take place in a public place.

117. A private members' club holds a 'stag' evening in a building the club owns. The intention is to have a dinner which will be followed by several female lap dancer acts—those attending have been promised by the organiser that the lap dancers will engage in sexual acts with men attending the event. Thirty men attend the event and during the evening they drink a large amount of alcohol meaning that they are all extremely drunk when HOPKINSON, the first lap dancer, takes the stage. Because of the conduct of the men, HOPKINSON runs off the stage and hides behind the bar. The group become agitated and all threaten violence towards HOPKINSON, demanding that she return to the stage and perform a sex act. TAWLEY, SMITH and OWEN are particularly nasty as they run behind the bar and physically drag HOPKINSON back to the stage, punching her several times in the process.

Has an offence of riot (contrary to s. 1 of the Public Order Act 1986) been committed in this situation?

A No, as riot cannot be committed in a private place—it can only be committed in public.
B Yes, but only TAWLEY, SMITH and OWEN are guilty of the offence.
C No, as only three persons used violence rather than 12 or more.
D Yes, all the men at the event commit the offence.

118. PC BAINES is on uniform patrol when he is approached by DONEGAN who tells the officer that he has just seen MATTHEWS driving a car at speed along a nearby road. DONEGAN states that he heard a loud bang as MATTHEWS drove along the road and thinks that MATTHEWS has struck a parked car. PC BAINES believes that an accident has taken place and several minutes later PC BAINES stops the car driven by MATTHEWS.

In relation to procedures following an accident (under s. 6(5) of the Road Traffic Act 1988), can PC BAINES require MATTHEWS to take a preliminary breath test?

A No, because an accident must have actually taken place. PC BAINES's belief that an accident has taken place is not enough to meet the requirement.
B Yes, but the preliminary breath test can only take place at or near the place where the requirement to cooperate with the test is imposed.
C No, as PC BAINES must believe or suspect that MATTHEWS has been drinking.
D Yes, but only if PC BAINES reasonably believes that MATTHEWS has failed to stop at the scene of an accident.

119. An allegation of misconduct has been made against PC INGLESON and it has been decided that the public interest, having regard to the nature of the allegation and several other relevant considerations, requires that PC INGLESON be suspended.

In relation to such a suspension, which of the following comments is correct?

A For the period of the suspension, PC INGLESON will continue to hold the office of constable.
B The use of a suspension must be reviewed at least every eight weeks.
C Suspension must be authorised by a senior officer (which is an officer holding a rank above that of assistant chief constable/commander).
D The Standards of Professional Behaviour continue to apply to police officers who are suspended from duty.

120. FORBES and her boyfriend, PRICE, are having a loud and prolonged dispute inside their home. The noise has disturbed several of their neighbours who have contacted the police. PC VESEY attends the scene and is let into the house by FORBES and led into the living room where PRICE is. In front of PRICE, FORBES tells the officer that she has discovered PRICE has been sleeping with other women and that she wants him out of her house (the house belongs to FORBES). PRICE responds by saying to FORBES, *'As soon as this copper has gone, I will smash everything of yours in this house!'*

With regard to the law relating to a breach of the peace, which of the following comments is true?

A PC VESEY cannot arrest PRICE for a breach of the peace because the threat to FORBES's property was made in private (FORBES's house).
B PC VESEY cannot arrest PRICE for breach of the peace because the threat was to harm a person's property and not to harm a person.
C PC VESEY can arrest PRICE for a breach of the peace and he could be detained at a police station until there is no further likelihood of a reoccurrence of the breach of the peace.
D PC VESEY can arrest PRICE for a breach of the peace and once he has been taken to a police station, he could be bailed to appear at court in relation to the charge.

121. INCE commits an offence under s. 4 of the Public Order Act 1986 (fear or provocation of violence). PC BAJWA (an officer in uniform) visits INCE's home address to speak with INCE. When INCE answers the front door and sees the officer, he shouts *'Fuck off!'* and slams the door in the officer's face. PC BAJWA reasonably believes that INCE is still on the premises and is considering his powers of entry to effect an arrest.

If PC BAJWA considers it necessary to arrest INCE, could the officer enter and search the premises in order to arrest INCE using his powers of entry under s. 17 of the Police and Criminal Evidence Act 1984?

A Yes, but this is only because the officer is in uniform.
B No, as the offence under s. 4 of the Public Order Act 1986 is triable summarily only (it is not an indictable offence).
C No, as INCE is not unlawfully at large and PC BAJWA is not in 'hot pursuit' of him.
D Yes, and force may be used in exercising the power where it is necessary to do so.

122. SHIPP and CHALLICE work on the same shift in a jewellery shop owned by AKERS. One afternoon, SHIPP sees CHALLICE behaving in a suspicious manner by fumbling around in her handbag and seemingly placing something in it that looks like a gold bangle. SHIPP suspects that CHALLICE has stolen an item of jewellery from the shop but is not sure. Several days later, PC EAGLE attends the jewellery shop and speaks to members of staff as AKERS has notified the police of a series of thefts from the shop. PC EAGLE speaks to the staff as a group and asks them if they have seen anything suspicious while working in the shop. SHIPP remembers CHALLICE's behaviour but remains silent when the question is posed to the group as he does not like the police and knows that CHALLICE is having some financial problems. PC EAGLE later speaks to the staff individually and asks SHIPP if he knows anything about the thefts—SHIPP replies that he has seen nothing that would help the police.

Does SHIPP commit an offence of assisting an offender (contrary to s. 4 of the Criminal Law Act 1967)?

A Yes, the offence is committed by SHIPP when he remains silent in response to the initial question posed to the group by PC EAGLE.
B No, the offence has not been committed by SHIPP as he is only suspicious that CHALLICE is guilty of theft from the shop.
C Yes, but only when he lies to the officer in response to a direct question when spoken to as an individual.
D No, as an offence of theft is not a 'relevant offence'.

123. For several weeks, residents of a small cul-de-sac have been having problems with a group of youths behaving in an anti-social manner resulting in the police being called to the cul-de-sac on several occasions. The last time this happened, STEDDING (aged 17 years) and HARRIS (aged 22 years) were both arrested and charged with an offence under s. 4A of the Public Order Act 1986 (intentionally causing harassment, alarm and distress). The residents of the cul-de-sac are understandably concerned about the possibility of continued bad behaviour by the group and have spoken with the officer in the case (PC GODDARD). One of the residents mentioned that the situation could be helped if STEDDING and HARRIS were made the subjects of a 'criminal behaviour order'.

Which of the following comments is correct in relation to such an order?

A A criminal behaviour order is an alternative to convicting a person of an offence.
B STEDDING (as a person under the age of 18 years) cannot be subject to a criminal behaviour order.
C If HARRIS were convicted of the offence, a criminal behaviour order can be made in relation to him; such an order could run for an indefinite period.
D The purpose of such an order against STEDDING and HARRIS would be to prevent them from engaging in violent behaviour.

124. DC SPURLING approaches her supervisor for some advice relating to covert human intelligence sources (CHIS). DC SPURLING has been approached by OTTER (aged 15 years) who has told the officer that he has high-quality information about the drug-dealing activities of his uncle (TURNER). TURNER lives 20 miles away from OTTER and his family but regularly visits OTTER's parents and boasts about how much money he is making from his drug-dealing activities. OTTER wants to provide the information to the police because he is disgusted by the behaviour of his uncle.

Could OTTER be authorised as a CHIS in these circumstances?

A Yes, although the authorisation would be for a maximum of four months (beginning on the day the authorisation is granted).

B No, as a child under the age of 16 cannot be authorised to carry out CHIS activity in any circumstances.

C Yes, although the authorisation would be for a maximum of one month (beginning on the day the authorisation is granted).

D No, as the conduct of a juvenile CHIS cannot involve that CHIS providing information about any member of his/her family.

125. PC ADAMIK is making enquiries in relation to an offence of burglary that occurred at 15 Hillside View. The officer visits 17 Hillside View (next door to the attacked premises) as this house has several CCTV cameras installed and, because of the position of the cameras, the officer believes that they will have recorded the burglary taking place and the recordings could be used in evidence. PC ADAMIK is invited into the house by the owner and occupier, FLACK. FLACK tells the officer that the camera recordings are stored on the hard drive of his personal computer but he is going to wipe the drive clean in the next few hours.

In relation to s. 19 of the Police and Criminal Evidence Act 1984 (the general power of seizure), which of the following statements is correct?

A PC ADAMIK can require the information on the hard drive to be produced in a form that can be taken away and in which it is visible and legible.

B PC ADAMIK can seize the computer (he only needs to suspect that there is evidence connected to the commission of an offence on the computer in order to do so).

C The s. 19 power cannot be used as the power relates solely to property that has been obtained in the commission of an offence.

D The s. 19 power cannot be used as the power of seizure it creates does not relate to information stored in electronic form.

126. CHAPMAN (who is 14 years of age) is convicted of theft. The court decides to use its powers under s. 8 of the Crime and Disorder Act 1998 to make a parenting order in respect of GIBSON who is the guardian of CHAPMAN. In addition to the parenting order and with GIBSON's consent, the court orders GIBSON to enter into a recognisance to take proper care of CHAPMAN and exercise proper control over him (using its powers under s. 376 of the Sentencing Act 2020).

Which of the following comments is correct in relation to the parenting order and the binding over of GIBSON?

A The only reason the court may make a parenting order is because CHAPMAN has been convicted of an offence.
B A parenting order will last for a period not exceeding 12 months.
C In relation to the bind over, the maximum duration of such a recognisance is two years.
D The court must issue a bind over to GIBSON as CHAPMAN has been convicted of an offence.

127. PC STAS is on uniform mobile patrol and checks a car driven by OWEN. The check reveals that there is no insurance in place for the car. PC STAS attempts to stop the car but it drives off at speed. PC STAS makes further enquiries regarding the car and establishes the address where the car is registered to OWEN. PC STAS visits the address two days later and sees the vehicle on the driveway of the address (a private dwelling).

Can PC STAS seize the car using the power under s. 165A of the Road Traffic Act 1988?

A No, as 48 hours have passed since the time the incident took place.
B Yes, and PC STAS may use reasonable force in order to do so.
C No, as it is on the driveway of a private dwelling.
D Yes, the car may be seized at any time within 72 hours following the incident.

128. BALL and six of his friends plan to attend a designated football match between Aston Villa and Arsenal at Villa Park (the home ground of Aston Villa). BALL hires a Ford Galaxy SMVR (which seats seven people including the driver) to transport them from London to Birmingham. BALL drives the vehicle and picks up his six friends outside a pub. HAMES (who is part of the group of six) places boxes containing cans of lager in the rear of the Ford Galaxy. KEASEY (also part of the group) is already drunk when the group are picked up by BALL. He climbs into the vehicle and falls asleep straight away. BALL is aware that the lager has been placed in the rear of the vehicle and that KEASEY is drunk. The group then set off to Birmingham.

Who, if anyone, has committed an offence under s. 1A of the Sporting Events (Control of Alcohol etc.) Act 1985 (alcohol on other vehicles)?

A The offence has not been committed in these circumstances.
B Only BALL commits the offence.
C BALL and HAMES commit the offence.
D BALL, HAMES and KEASEY commit the offence.

129. PC WILLOUGHBY is accompanied by PANNELL (an approved mental health professional) and KOUSAR (a registered medical practitioner) when executing a warrant granted under s. 135(1) of the Mental Health Act 1983 at premises owned by McAULEY (who is a person believed to be suffering from a mental disorder). McAULEY is detained at the premises. PC WILLOUGHBY reasonably believes that McAULEY may present a danger to others and is concealing an item on his person that could be used to cause physical injury to others and is considering using the power under s. 136C of the Mental Health Act 1986 to search McAULEY.

In relation to that power, which of the following comments is correct?

A PC WILLOUGHBY, PANNELL or KOUSAR could search McAULEY using the power under s. 136C.
B The search authorises the removal of all items of clothing except those that would expose intimate body parts.
C The power cannot be used when executing a warrant (the power of search relates to a situation where a police officer removes a person to a place of safety under s. 136 of the Act).
D The power authorises PC WILLOUGHBY to search McAULEY's mouth.

130. PC BURCHILL attends a cinema where the manager reports that an offence of theft has taken place (£500 cash has been stolen) and that STEER (who works at the cinema) is responsible. When PC BURCHILL arrives, he is shown into a room where STEER is standing next to the manager and, as the officer walks in, STEER puts his hand into his trouser pocket and produces the stolen £500, saying *'I'm sorry I stole this.'* PC BURCHILL decides that an arrest is necessary to enable a 'special warning' to be given to STEER about the incriminating £500 and says, *'You're nicked for theft of the £500 from this cinema.'*

Considering Code G of the Codes of Practice and the law regarding arrest, which of the following statements is correct?

A 'Necessity' would not be satisfied on the basis that a suspect needed to be given a 'special warning' regarding possession of incriminating objects (the £500).
B STEER must be informed of the reason why the arrest is considered necessary.
C Failing to use the word 'arrest' when arresting STEER means this is an unlawful arrest.
D There was no need for PC BURCHILL to provide grounds for the arrest as it was obvious why the arrest was being made.

131. PC DUFFY is subject to a complaint and the investigation of the complaint has led to a misconduct meeting taking place.

In relation to that misconduct meeting, and in particular the timing of the misconduct meeting, which of the following comments is correct?

A The misconduct meeting shall take place not later than 20 working days beginning with the first working day after the date on which the documents and material for the meeting were supplied to PC DUFFY; this time limit may not be extended.
B The misconduct meeting shall take place not later than 28 working days beginning with the first working day after the date on which the documents and material for the meeting were supplied to PC DUFFY; this time limit may not be extended.
C The misconduct meeting shall take place not later than 20 working days beginning with the first working day after the date on which the documents and material for the meeting were supplied to PC DUFFY; this time limit may be extended.
D The misconduct meeting shall take place not later than 28 working days beginning with the first working day after the date on which the documents and material for the meeting were supplied to PC DUFFY; this time limit may be extended.

132. DC JELF is investigating an offence of sexual assault (under s. 3 of the Sexual Offences Act 2003) that took place in Wood Street last Saturday evening. The officer believes that there may well be a number of untraced witnesses to the offence and wishes to identify them by carrying out a road check (under s. 4 of the Police and Criminal Evidence Act 1984) in Wood Street this coming Saturday evening. DC JELF approaches Inspector VIVIER and asks for his authorisation for a road check to take place.

Can Inspector VIVIER authorise a road check in these circumstances?

A No, as a road check cannot be authorised to ascertain whether a vehicle is carrying a witness to an indictable offence, only a person who has committed such an offence.
B Yes, and if authorised it will last for a period not exceeding seven days.
C No, it must be authorised by an officer of the rank of superintendent or above.
D Yes, but the authorisation must be in writing.

133. PC CURTIS is on uniform foot patrol when she is directed to an incident involving an offence of assault. PC CURTIS arrives at the scene of the offence and, as a result of information received, she arrests HYNDE on suspicion of committing assault. As PC CURTIS is on her own, she asks for another officer to attend the scene but is informed that no other officers are available to do so. The officer is concerned that she will not be able to take HYNDE to a designated police station without HYNDE injuring her so she decides to take HYNDE to a non-designated police station which is a three-minute walk from the scene of the arrest.

Considering s. 30 of the Police and Criminal Evidence Act 1984, which of the following comments is correct?

A The officer has behaved unlawfully as all arrested persons must be taken to a designated police station as soon as practicable after the arrest. There are no exceptions to this requirement.

B The behaviour of PC CURTIS is lawful but HYNDE should be taken to a designated police station not more than six hours after his arrival at the first police station unless he is released previously.

C The officer has behaved unlawfully as the only justification for taking an arrested person to a non-designated police station after arrest is if it appears to the constable that the arrested person will injure him/herself, the constable or some other person.

D The behaviour of PC CURTIS is lawful as long as, after arriving at the non-designated police station, she contacts an officer of the rank of inspector or above to inform him/her of her actions. In such a case, the arrested person will be taken to a designated police station as soon as is practicable.

134. DYKE has been arrested in connection with an offence of driving a motor vehicle while over the prescribed limit (contrary to s. 5(1)(a) of the Road Traffic Act 1988). DYKE was required to provide evidential specimens of breath at a police station, both of which were over the prescribed alcohol limit. DYKE has been charged with the offence.

Could DYKE be detained at the police station using the power under s. 10 of the Road Traffic Act 1988 (detention of person affected)?

A Yes, if a constable has reasonable grounds for suspecting that were DYKE to drive a motor vehicle on a road he would commit an offence under s. 5 or 5A of the Road Traffic Act 1988.

B No, not unless a constable has consulted a medical practitioner regarding DYKE's ability to drive and that practitioner states that DYKE's ability to drive would be impaired.

C Yes, if a constable has reasonable grounds for believing that were DYKE to drive a mechanically propelled vehicle on a road he would commit an offence under s. 4, 5 or 5A of the Road Traffic Act 1988.

D No, as DYKE has not been arrested and charged with an offence under s. 5A of the Road Traffic Act 1988 (driving, attempting to drive or being in charge of a motor vehicle with a concentration of a specified drug above a specified limit).

135. A house situated at 239 Main Road has been the subject of a number of calls to the police over the past 24 hours. This started off with complaints about noise but has now escalated and the last call resulted in the police attending the scene and a number of arrests being made for drug-related offences directly outside the house. Inspector CRACKNELL is satisfied, on reasonable grounds, that if a closure notice (under s. 76 of the Anti-social Behaviour, Crime and Disorder Act 2014) is not issued then it is likely that there will soon be disorder near the house associated with the use of the house and a closure notice is necessary to prevent the disorder occurring.

In relation to such a closure notice, which of the following comments is correct?

A Inspector CRACKNELL may issue the closure notice; the maximum period that can be specified in the notice is 24 hours.
B Inspector CRACKNELL may issue the closure notice; the maximum period that can be specified in the notice is 48 hours.
C Inspector CRACKNELL cannot issue the notice as the relevant rank to issue a closure notice is an officer of the rank of at least superintendent.
D Inspector CRACKNELL cannot issue a closure notice as there has been no disorder at the premises.

136. PC CULPAN (a female officer) and PC KHAN (a male officer) stop FRASER in a public place and search him under s. 23 of the Misuse of Drugs Act 1971. During the search, PC CULPAN places her hands inside the pockets of a coat FRASER is wearing. Nothing is found during a cursory search but the officers decide a more thorough search is required and they take FRASER into a police van (the inside of which cannot be seen by the public). Inside the van, PC KHAN requires FRASER to remove his headwear and then PC CULPAN requires FRASER to remove his shoes. The officers find nothing during the course of the search—they make a record of the search and FRASER leaves.

Which of the following statements is correct?

A PC CULPAN should not have placed her hands into FRASER's coat.
B The search could have taken place at a police station or other location out of public view but not a police vehicle.
C PC CULPAN should not have been present in the police vehicle when FRASER was required to remove his headgear.
D There was nothing wrong with PC CULPAN asking FRASER to remove his shoes.

137. LORIMER is a Police Community Support Officer visiting a newsagents owned by GRACE who has complained about anti-social behaviour in the area. LORIMER is chatting to GRACE in the shop when she sees YORK acting in a very odd way in the shop. LORIMER forms the suspicion that YORK is committing an offence of theft and decides to arrest YORK using the power of arrest available under s. 24A of the Police and Criminal Evidence Act 1984. When LORIMER is later asked why she arrested YORK, she states that it was not reasonably practicable for a constable to make the arrest instead of her and she had reasonable grounds to believe that YORK would make off before a constable could assume responsibility for him.

Considering the power of arrest under s. 24A of the Police and Criminal Evidence Act 1984, which of the following comments is correct?

A LORIMER should not have arrested YORK as the power of arrest under s. 24A is not available to a Police Community Support Officer.

B In this situation, LORIMER has acted correctly and this is a lawful arrest.

C As theft is triable either way, this is an unlawful arrest (the power can only be exercised in relation to an indictable offence).

D This is an unlawful arrest as the power can only be used where the person reasonably believes (not suspects) that a person is committing an indictable offence.

138. PCs PRENTICE and FELLOWES are on uniform mobile patrol when they are called to a disturbance outside a pub. When they arrive, VICKER is standing outside the pub shouting and swearing very loudly. The officers cannot calm VICKER down and have no choice but to arrest him for a public order offence. On arrest, VICKER becomes extremely violent towards the officers and is resisting the arrest with all his might. The incident has drawn a crowd of 10 people from the pub. In the crowd are HARLOW and GREEN who both hate the police. While VICKER struggles, HARLOW shouts out *'We'll help you mate, we'll kick their fuckin' heads in!'* and GREEN kicks out at PC FELLOWES but misses. He kicks out again but this time at the door of the police vehicle the officers arrived in and he dents the door. Other officers arrive and VICKER is taken from the scene. HARLOW and GREEN are also arrested. All three men are later charged with the offence of violent disorder (contrary to s. 2 of the Public Order Act 1986).

Which of the following statements is correct?

A The offence of violent disorder has been committed by all three men in this scenario.

B The offence has not been committed as the three men did not act deliberately in combination with each other.

C The offence of violent disorder has not been committed as GREEN's conduct was towards property not a person and this does not satisfy the requirement for 'unlawful violence'.

D The offence has not been committed as three or more people must actually use violence for a conviction to be secured.

139. A protest is to take place regarding immigration. A large amount of intelligence has been received about the protest which includes information to the effect that a number of the protesters will be wearing masks and other items to wholly or mainly conceal their identity, enabling them to commit offences without being identified. At a similar protest march a few weeks earlier, several public order and assault offences took place and the offenders all wore items concealing their identity. As a result of this information, an authorisation under s. 60AA of the Criminal Justice and Public Order Act 1994 is given.

In relation to such an authorisation, which of the following comments is correct?

A The initial authorisation will last for a maximum period of 12 hours.
B The power under s. 60AA is only available to police officers in uniform.
C The power under s. 60AA allows police officers to search persons and vehicles for items that might be used wholly or mainly to conceal identity.
D After the initial authorisation period has ended, the power cannot be extended.

140. Inspector THOMAS is delivering a training course for newly promoted sergeants and inspectors—part of the course deals with the law in relation to the Equality Act 2010 and in particular the 'protected characteristics' covered by the Act. During a class discussion in relation to those protected characteristics and case law surrounding the issue, a number of comments are made.

In relation to the comments made by members of the class, which one shows a correct understanding of Equality Act 2010 law?

A When discussing the protected characteristic of disability (s. 6 of the Act), a member of the class states that people who have a disability are protected against discrimination; those who have had a disability are not protected.
B When discussing the protected characteristic of religion or belief (s. 10 of the Act), a member of the class states that a person holding gender-critical beliefs (that sex is immutable) would have this characteristic.
C When discussing the protected characteristic of marriage and civil partnership (s. 8 of the Act), a member of the class states that opposite-sex couples in a civil partnership do not have this characteristic.
D When discussing the protected characteristic of race (s. 9 of the Act), a member of the class states that as Scots, Welsh and English persons are ethnic groups, they would have this characteristic.

141. HEMMING is the licensee of 'The Crooked Man' pub. It is his birthday and, when the pub is closed, he has a private celebration in the lounge of the pub with his best friend WILLIAMSON. The two men become exceptionally drunk and use a karaoke machine so loudly that neighbours complain and the police are called to the pub. PC WHITE attends the pub and finds the two men in the lounge of the pub, drunk and singing loudly.

Has the offence of being found drunk (contrary to s. 12 of the Licensing Act 1872) been committed in these circumstances?

A Yes, but only WILLIAMSON would commit the offence in these circumstances.
B No, as this offence only applies to licensed premises when they are open to the public.
C Yes, HEMMING and WILLIAMSON have committed the offence.
D No, as the men are not found drunk in any highway or public place.

142. HODGSON is driving a Land Rover motor vehicle and towing a caravan. He drives onto a field owned by EGERTON and sets up to camp on the field (trespassing in the field). EGERTON sees this and contacts the police and PC YASAR (an officer on uniform patrol) attends the scene where EGERTON asks the officer to remove HODGSON from his land. PC YASAR speaks to HODGSON who tells the officer that he is from the travelling community and intends to camp on the land for three days. PC YASAR establishes that there is a suitable pitch on a relevant caravan site for HODGSON's caravan at a nearby local authority camping site.

Can PC YASAR direct HODGSON to leave the site using the power under s. 62A of the Criminal Justice and Public Order Act 1994?

A Yes, but only because the officer is in uniform.
B No, EGERTON has not taken reasonable steps to ask HODGSON to leave.
C Yes, if an inspector or above authorises it, the direction to leave can be communicated by any constable at the scene.
D No, as there is only one person (HODGSON) trespassing on the land.

143. PC REED has been a police officer for seven years and lives with LEEDHAM (who lives with PC REED as if she were his spouse). LEEDHAM and PC REED's father (who does not live with PC REED) decide to go into business together running a social club (LEEDHAM will hold the alcohol licence for the premises and PC REED's father will have a pecuniary interest in it). PC REED approaches his supervisor (PS LANGTREE) for some advice regarding whether he needs to inform the chief officer of police about the proposed 'business interest' of his relatives with the social club.

Considering the content of reg. 7 and the requirements of reg. 8 of the Police Regulations 2003, which of the following comments is correct?

A There is no need to inform the chief officer of police regarding the activities of LEEDHAM and PC REED's father as they have occurred 'post' (seven years after) the officer joining the police.
B Regulation 8 does not require notification of a business interest of a 'relative'; this would only be relevant if the officer themselves proposed to run a business.
C PC REED needs to notify the chief officer of police regarding the proposed business interest of LEEDHAM and his father.
D PC REED needs to notify the chief officer of police about the proposed business interest of LEEDHAM but not that of his father.

144. PC MONTIERO is on uniform mobile patrol when she is sent to a disturbance outside a council building. When the officer arrives, she is spoken to by WRAGG who tells the officer that a few moments before the officer arrived a group of people shouting and using extreme political language had been causing trouble outside the council building. One of them had dropped a bag outside the council building and told WRAGG that it contained an explosive. PC MONTIERO believes the situation is 'urgent' and is considering whether she can designate an area around the bag as a 'cordoned area' under ss. 33 to 36 of the Terrorism Act 2000.

Could PC MONTIERO make such a designation?

A No, such a designation can only be made by an officer of the rank of inspector or above.
B No, such a designation can only be made by an officer of the rank of assistant chief constable (or commander) or above.
C Yes, but it cannot be given orally, it must be in writing.
D Yes, and PC MONTIERO must ensure an officer of the rank of superintendent or above is informed of the designation.

145. PC BARROWCLOUGH receives information that stolen property is being stored in three separate houses all owned by HIPGRAVE. The officer applies to a justice of the peace for a search warrant under s. 8 of the Police and Criminal Evidence Act 1984 to search the three premises and is granted a 'specific premises warrant' to search the three houses. The warrant authorises an unlimited number of entries to the premises.

According to s. 15 of the Police and Criminal Evidence Act 1984, how many copies of such a warrant will be made?

A One copy will be made of the warrant.
B Two copies will be made of the warrant.
C A copy will be made for every separate premises to be entered (in this case, that will be three copies).
D As many copies as are reasonably required may be made of the warrant.

146. An authorisation for officers to utilise the powers of stop and search in a specific location (under s. 47A of the Terrorism Act 2000) has been given. PC BUCHANAN is on uniform mobile patrol in the area where the authorisation is active and is following a vehicle driven by SNOOKS. PC BUCHANAN decides to stop and search the vehicle and SNOOKS for the purpose of discovering whether there is anything which may constitute evidence that the vehicle is being used for the purposes of terrorism or if SNOOKS is a terrorist. During the course of the search, PC BUCHANAN forms the reasonable suspicion that SNOOKS is a terrorist and arrests SNOOKS on that basis under s. 41 of the Terrorism Act 2000.

In relation to the behaviour of the officer, which of the following comments is correct?

A PC BUCHANAN correctly stopped the vehicle but has unlawfully arrested SNOOKS.
B PC BUCHANAN correctly stopped the vehicle and the arrest of SNOOKS was lawful.
C PC BUCHANAN could not stop the vehicle under s. 47A of the Terrorism Act 2000 (the officer should have used the general power to stop a vehicle under s. 163 of the Road Traffic Act 1988 and then searched SNOOKS).
D PC BUCHANAN could not stop the vehicle under s. 47A of the Terrorism Act 2000 unless he reasonably believed that the vehicle was being used for terrorist purposes.

147. A number of public order incidents have occurred outside a house owned by COSTELLO due to a rumour that he has had a lottery win in excess of £50 million—this is not true. However, the rumour is being repeated on social media and the police are concerned that this will result in significant amounts of anti-social behaviour taking place outside COSTELLO's house. Consideration is being given to authorising the use of the dispersal power under s. 34 of the Anti-social Behaviour, Crime and Policing Act 2014 in order to remove or reduce the likelihood of anti-social behaviour occurring.

In relation to such an authorisation and the powers that are associated with it, which of the following comments is correct?

A If a person is directed to leave under such an authorisation, that direction must be given in writing to ensure that the person is clear where they are being dispersed from.
B A person directed to leave a specified area subject to the authorisation can be directed not to return for a specified period of up to 72 hours.
C If authorised, the dispersal power is available to constables in uniform; it is not available to police community support officers.
D The authorisation can only be given by a police officer of at least the rank of inspector.

148. PC KERSLAKE (who is on uniform mobile patrol) has attended the scene of an accident where two motor vehicles collided with each other. The officer required the drivers of both vehicles to take part in a preliminary breath test; PENNY (the driver of one of the vehicles) failed that test.

With regard to the requirement for an evidential breath specimen from PENNY (under s. 7 of the Road Traffic Act 1988), which of the following statements is correct?

A PC KERSLAKE could only make this requirement at a police station.
B PC KERSLAKE could only make this requirement at a police station or at a hospital.
C PC KERSLAKE could make this requirement at a police station, a hospital or other medical premises.
D PC KERSLAKE can make the requirement at or near the place where the preliminary breath test has been administered to PENNY.

149. ANDERSON is outside a shopping centre and is behaving in a very strange way, so much so that the police have been called as there are concerns about ANDERSON. PCs GOATLEY and YOUNG arrive and speak to ANDERSON who shouts at the officers, *'You are all agents of the evil one and I shall destroy you with my wand of fire!'* whilst waving a wooden stick at the officers. It appears to the officers that ANDERSON is suffering from a mental disorder and is in immediate need of care and control so they detain him under s. 136 of the Mental Health Act 1983.

In relation to the power under s. 136 of the Act, which of the following comments is correct?

A ANDERSON should be taken to a place of safety but under no circumstances should this be a police station.

B The decision to use a police station as a place of safety must be authorised by an officer of the rank of inspector or above.

C The maximum time a person removed to a place of safety can be detained for cannot exceed 72 hours.

D If ANDERSON is taken to a place of safety by the police, he will be considered to be in 'police detention'.

150. Serious disorder takes place at a pub and several people are stabbed. Inspector BRANNAN authorises the use of the power under s. 60 of the Criminal Justice and Public Order Act 1994 in response to the incident. A significant number of police officers are at the scene including PC MAKIN (in uniform) and DC VERNEY (who is dressed in plain clothes). The two officers are chatting when FUREY walks by them wearing a baseball cap on his head and a scarf over his face so that only his eyes can be seen. Both officers reasonably believe FUREY is wearing the cap and scarf to conceal his identity.

Which of the following comments is correct?

A Only PC MAKIN could require FUREY to remove the baseball cap and scarf.

B PC MAKIN or DC VERNEY could require FUREY to remove the baseball cap and scarf.

C Neither officer could require the removal of the baseball cap and scarf.

D PC MAKIN or DC VERNEY could require FUREY to remove the baseball cap and scarf and also search FUREY for other items that could be used to conceal his identity.

Marking instructions

- Mark like this ~~A~~
- Make no stray marks
- Please do **NOT** tick, cross or circle

Answer Sheet

OXFORD
UNIVERSITY PRESS

Blackstone's Police Sergeants' and Inspectors' Mock Examination Paper 2025

1	A	B	C	D	51	A	B	C	D	101	A	B	C	D
2	A	B	C	D	52	A	B	C	D	102	A	B	C	D
3	A	B	C	D	53	A	B	C	D	103	A	B	C	D
4	A	B	C	D	54	A	B	C	D	104	A	B	C	D
5	A	B	C	D	55	A	B	C	D	105	A	B	C	D
6	A	B	C	D	56	A	B	C	D	106	A	B	C	D
7	A	B	C	D	57	A	B	C	D	107	A	B	C	D
8	A	B	C	D	58	A	B	C	D	108	A	B	C	D
9	A	B	C	D	59	A	B	C	D	109	A	B	C	D
10	A	B	C	D	60	A	B	C	D	110	A	B	C	D
11	A	B	C	D	61	A	B	C	D	111	A	B	C	D
12	A	B	C	D	62	A	B	C	D	112	A	B	C	D
13	A	B	C	D	63	A	B	C	D	113	A	B	C	D
14	A	B	C	D	64	A	B	C	D	114	A	B	C	D
15	A	B	C	D	65	A	B	C	D	115	A	B	C	D
16	A	B	C	D	66	A	B	C	D	116	A	B	C	D
17	A	B	C	D	67	A	B	C	D	117	A	B	C	D
18	A	B	C	D	68	A	B	C	D	118	A	B	C	D
19	A	B	C	D	69	A	B	C	D	119	A	B	C	D
20	A	B	C	D	70	A	B	C	D	120	A	B	C	D
21	A	B	C	D	71	A	B	C	D	121	A	B	C	D
22	A	B	C	D	72	A	B	C	D	122	A	B	C	D
23	A	B	C	D	73	A	B	C	D	123	A	B	C	D
24	A	B	C	D	74	A	B	C	D	124	A	B	C	D
25	A	B	C	D	75	A	B	C	D	125	A	B	C	D
26	A	B	C	D	76	A	B	C	D	126	A	B	C	D
27	A	B	C	D	77	A	B	C	D	127	A	B	C	D
28	A	B	C	D	78	A	B	C	D	128	A	B	C	D
29	A	B	C	D	79	A	B	C	D	129	A	B	C	D
30	A	B	C	D	80	A	B	C	D	130	A	B	C	D
31	A	B	C	D	81	A	B	C	D	131	A	B	C	D
32	A	B	C	D	82	A	B	C	D	132	A	B	C	D
33	A	B	C	D	83	A	B	C	D	133	A	B	C	D
34	A	B	C	D	84	A	B	C	D	134	A	B	C	D
35	A	B	C	D	85	A	B	C	D	135	A	B	C	D
36	A	B	C	D	86	A	B	C	D	136	A	B	C	D
37	A	B	C	D	87	A	B	C	D	137	A	B	C	D
38	A	B	C	D	88	A	B	C	D	138	A	B	C	D
39	A	B	C	D	89	A	B	C	D	139	A	B	C	D
40	A	B	C	D	90	A	B	C	D	140	A	B	C	D
41	A	B	C	D	91	A	B	C	D	141	A	B	C	D
42	A	B	C	D	92	A	B	C	D	142	A	B	C	D
43	A	B	C	D	93	A	B	C	D	143	A	B	C	D
44	A	B	C	D	94	A	B	C	D	144	A	B	C	D
45	A	B	C	D	95	A	B	C	D	145	A	B	C	D
46	A	B	C	D	96	A	B	C	D	146	A	B	C	D
47	A	B	C	D	97	A	B	C	D	147	A	B	C	D
48	A	B	C	D	98	A	B	C	D	148	A	B	C	D
49	A	B	C	D	99	A	B	C	D	149	A	B	C	D
50	A	B	C	D	100	A	B	C	D	150	A	B	C	D

OXFORD
UNIVERSITY PRESS

Blackstone's Police Sergeants' and Inspectors' Mock Examination Paper 2025

Pack 2

Contents

DO NOT OPEN THIS ANSWER PACK UNTIL YOU HAVE COMPLETED THE MOCK EXAM

OXFORD UNIVERSITY PRESS	**Blackstone's Police Sergeants' and Inspectors' Mock Examination Paper 2025**

Marking Instructions

Lay your answer sheet next to the marking matrix and begin the marking process.

Starting with Question 1, compare your marked answer with the correct answer given in the marking matrix. If the correct answer matches your marked answer put a '✓' mark inside the white box on the relevant row (see questions 1 to 4 below). If it does not (see Question 3) put an '✗' mark.

Question	Answer	Crime	Random Non-counting MCQ
1	B	✓	
2	A	✓	
3	D	✗	
4	A	✓	

The first 60 questions in the Mock Examination all relate to the Crime element of the syllabus; however, you will see that not all of the 60 questions will count towards your mark as 3 questions within this block of 60 have been designated as a 'Random Non-counting MCQ'—this means for the Crime section of the examination you will actually be marked out of a total of 57. This is in order to reflect the nature of the marking process used in your NPPF Step 2 Legal Examination.

When you have marked the Crime questions, add up the total (out of 35 and 22) to give you a mark out of 57 (in the following example the total is 39/57).

35	C	✓	
36	A	✗	
Total	=	21/35	

59	C	✓	
60	C	✗	
Total	=	18/22	

Then do the same for Questions 61 to 92 ('Evidence and Procedure') and Questions 93 to 150 ('General Police Duties').

Enter the totals for each block of questions in the 'Final Score' table and add them up to reach a final total (out of 140) for the whole exam.

Compare your final score to the table underneath the 'Final Score', which will indicate whether or not you have passed the mock examination.

The pass mark for the sergeants' examination is 77 (55%).

The pass mark for the inspectors' examination is 91 (65%).

Marking Matrix, Questions 1–36 (Crime)

Question	Answer	Crime	Random Non-counting MCQ
1	B		
2	A		
3	D		
4	A		
5	C		
6	D		
7	B		
8	C		
9	C		
10	A		
11	C		
12	A		
13	B		
14	C		
15	B		
16	B		
17	A		
18	A		
19	A		
20	D		
21	A		
22	B		
23	D		
24	D		
25	A		
26	C		
27	B		
28	B		
29	C		
30	A		
31	C		
32	D		
33	D		
34	D		
35	C		
36	A		
Total	=	/35	

Marking Matrix, Questions 37–60 (Crime)

Question	Answer	Crime	Random Non-counting MCQ
37	A		
38	B		
39	B		
40	C		
41	C		
42	B		
43	A		
44	C		
45	A		
46	C		
47	B		
48	A		
49	A		
50	B		
51	D		
52	A		
53	A		
54	C		
55	B		
56	C		
57	D		
58	C		
59	C		
60	C		
Total	=	/22	

Marking Matrix, Questions 61–92 (Evidence and Procedure)

Question	Answer	Evidence and Procedure	Random Non-counting MCQ
61	B		
62	A		
63	A		
64	B		
65	C		
66	C		
67	D		
68	D		
69	B		
70	C		
71	A		
72	C		
73	B		
74	B		
75	D		
76	C		
77	C		
78	B		
79	B		
80	A		
81	B		
82	C		
83	D		
84	A		
85	D		
86	B		
87	C		
88	C		
89	B		
90	C		
91	D		
92	D		
Total	=	/29	

Marking Matrix, Questions 93–128 (General Police Duties)

Question	Answer	General Police Duties	Random Non-counting MCQ
93	D		
94	B		
95	B		
96	A		
97	D		
98	C		
99	B		
100	C		
101	D		
102	C		
103	A		
104	C		
105	B		
106	B		
107	C		
108	A		
109	D		
110	C		
111	C		
112	C		
113	D		
114	A		
115	A		
116	B		
117	B		
118	A		
119	D		
120	C		
121	D		
122	B		
123	C		
124	A		
125	A		
126	B		
127	A		
128	A		
Total	=	/34	

Marking Matrix, Questions 129–150 (General Police Duties)

Question	Answer	General Police Duties	Random Non-counting MCQ
129	D		
130	B		
131	C		
132	C		
133	B		
134	C		
135	A		
136	D		
137	B		
138	A		
139	B		
140	B		
141	C		
142	D		
143	C		
144	D		
145	D		
146	B		
147	D		
148	D		
149	B		
150	A		
Total	=	/20	

Final Score

Syllabus Area	*Marks*
Crime	**/57**
Evidence and Procedure	**/29**
General Police Duties	**/54**
TOTAL =	**/140**

Questions right	% score	Questions right	% score	Questions right	% score	Questions right	% score	Questions right	% score
1	0.714	29	20.714	57	40.714	85	60.714	113	80.714
2	1.428	30	21.428	58	41.428	86	61.428	114	81.428
3	2.142	31	22.142	59	42.142	87	62.142	115	82.142
4	2.857	32	22.857	60	42.857	88	62.857	116	82.857
5	3.571	33	23.571	61	43.571	89	63.571	117	83.571
6	4.285	34	24.285	62	44.285	90	64.285	118	84.285
7	5	35	25	63	45	91	65 (pass)	119	85
8	5.714	36	25.714	64	45.714	92	65.714	120	85.714
9	6.428	37	26.428	65	46.428	93	66.428	121	86.428
10	7.142	38	27.142	66	47.142	94	67.142	122	87.142
11	7.857	39	27.857	67	47.857	95	67.857	123	87.857
12	8.571	40	28.571	68	48.571	96	68.571	124	88.571
13	9.285	41	29.285	69	49.285	97	69.285	125	89.285
14	10	42	30	70	50	98	70	126	90
15	10.714	43	30.714	71	50.714	99	70.714	127	90.714
16	11.428	44	31.428	72	51.428	100	71.428	128	91.428
17	12.142	45	32.142	73	52.142	101	72.142	129	92.142
18	12.857	46	32.857	74	52.857	102	72.857	130	92.857
19	13.571	47	33.571	75	53.571	103	73.571	131	93.571
20	14.285	48	34.285	76	54.285	104	74.285	132	94.285
21	15	49	35	77	55 (pass)	105	75	133	95
22	15.714	50	35.714	78	55.714	106	75.714	134	95.714
23	16.428	51	36.428	79	56.428	107	76.428	135	96.428
24	17.142	52	37.142	80	57.142	108	77.142	136	97.142
25	17.857	53	37.857	81	57.857	109	77.857	137	97.857
26	18.571	54	38.571	82	58.571	110	78.571	138	98.571
27	19.285	55	39.285	83	59.285	111	79.285	139	99.285
28	20	56	40	84	60	112	80	140	100

OXFORD
UNIVERSITY PRESS

Blackstone's Police Sergeants' and Inspectors' Mock Examination Paper 2025

Answer Booklet

1. Answer **B** — Section 28 of the Violent Crime Reduction Act 2006 states:

   (1) A person is guilty of an offence if—
   (a) he uses another to look after, hide or transport a dangerous weapon for him; and
   (b) he does so under arrangements or in circumstances that facilitate, or are intended to facilitate, the weapon's being available to him for an unlawful purpose.
   (2) For the purposes of this section the cases in which a dangerous weapon is to be regarded as available to a person for an unlawful purpose include any case where—
   (a) the weapon is available for him to take possession of it at a time and place; and
   (b) his possession of the weapon at that time and place would constitute, or be likely to involve or to lead to, the commission by him of an offence.

   It appears, on the face of it, that DAVENPORT has committed the offence. However, a 'dangerous weapon' means a firearm other than an air weapon or a component part of, or accessory to, an air weapon; or a weapon to which s. 141 or 141A of the Criminal Justice Act 1988 applies. So whilst the offence does relate to firearms (making answer A incorrect), it does not relate to air weapons (making answers C and D incorrect).

   Crime, para. 1.7.9.6

2. Answer **A** — Section 71(2) of the Domestic Abuse Act 2021 states that it is *not a defence* that the victim of a 'relevant offence' consented to the infliction of the serious harm for the purposes of obtaining sexual gratification. A 'relevant offence' means an offence under s. 18, 20 or 47 of the Offences Against the Person Act 1861.

   'Serious harm' means:

   - grievous bodily harm, within the meaning of s. 18 of the 1861 Act;
   - wounding, within the meaning of that section; or
   - actual bodily harm, within the meaning of s. 47 of the 1861 Act.

   Section 71(2) would be relevant to all the offences committed but the question specifically asks at what point would that *first* be the case—that is when the s. 47 offence is committed (correct answer A).

   Crime, para. 1.10.5.3

3. Answer **D** — Section 23(2) of the Misuse of Drugs Act 1971 states that if a constable has reasonable grounds to suspect (not believe—answer A is incorrect) that any person is in possession of a controlled drug in contravention of this Act or of any regulations or orders made thereunder, the constable may: (a) search that person, and detain him for the purpose of searching him; (b) search any vehicle or vessel in which the constable suspects that the drug may be found, and for that purpose require the person in control of the vehicle or vessel to stop it (answer B is incorrect); and (c) seize and detain, for the purposes of proceedings under this Act, anything found in the course of the search which appears to the constable to be evidence of an offence under this Act. The power under s. 23(2) can be used anywhere (answer C is incorrect—see *General Police Duties*, para. 3.1.8 (Annex A)).

Crime, para. 1.6.15.1

4. Answer **A** — Establishing a causal link may be relatively straightforward in many cases, e.g. a defendant throws a brick at a window and the window is broken by the brick hitting it; the window would not have broken 'but for' the defendant's conduct. Where the link becomes more difficult to prove is when the defendant's behaviour triggers other events or aggravates existing circumstances. This MCQ is an example of such a situation and closely follows the circumstances of case law in the decision in *R* v *McKechnie* [1992] Crim LR 194. In that case, the defendant attacked the victim, who was already suffering from a serious ulcer, causing him brain damage. The brain damage (caused by the assault) prevented doctors from operating on the ulcer which eventually ruptured, killing the victim. The Court of Appeal, upholding the conviction for manslaughter, held that the defendant's criminal conduct (the assault) had made a significant contribution to the victim's death even though the untreated ulcer was the actual cause of death (correct answer A), therefore answers C and D are incorrect. Answer B is incorrect as the chain of causation can be broken, for example by an intervening act.

Crime, para. 1.2.6

5. Answer **C** — If a defendant intended to kill or cause serious injury to the mother, that intention cannot support a charge of murder in respect of the baby if it goes on to die after being born alive (making answers A and D incorrect). It may, however, support a charge of manslaughter (*Attorney-General's Reference (No. 3 of 1994)* [1998] AC 245). However that does not make B correct—answer B states that WINDEBANK could only ever be charged with manslaughter and that is not correct as it would certainly be appropriate to charge a person with the murder of the child if he/she intended the child to die after having been born alive (correct answer C).

Crime, para. 1.5.2

6. Answer **D** — The Sexual Offences Act 2003, s. 2 states:

(1) A person (A) commits an offence if—
   (a) he intentionally penetrates the vagina or anus of another person (B) with a part of his body or anything else,
   (b) the penetration is sexual,
   (c) B does not consent to the penetration, and
   (d) A does not reasonably believe that B consents.

The penetration must be of the victim's vagina or anus—these activities would not amount to an offence under s. 2 of the Act.

Crime, para. 1.12.4.1

7. Answer **B** — Section 46 of the Children Act 1989 states:

   (1) Where a constable has reasonable cause to believe that a child would otherwise be likely to suffer significant harm, he may—
      (a) remove the child to suitable accommodation and keep him there; or
      (b) take such steps as are reasonable to ensure the child's removal from any hospital, or other place, in which he is then being accommodated is prevented.

   A 'child' is someone who is under 18 years old (s. 105), so CAMPBELL is classed as a 'child' and answer A is incorrect. There is no requirement for an 'authorising officer'—the power is available to a constable, making answer C incorrect. The 'designated officer' in a police protection matter has a number of duties to fulfil but the 'initiating officer' (PC GINN) and the 'designated officer' must not carry out the two separate roles, meaning that answer D is incorrect. The longest a child can spend in 'police protection' is 72 hours (correct answer B).

   Crime, para. 1.13.4

8. Answer **C** — The Sexual Offences Act 2003, s. 66 states:

   (1) A person commits an offence if—
      (a) he intentionally exposes his genitals, and
      (b) he intends that someone will see them and be caused alarm or distress.

   The offence can be committed in public or private and there is no requirement that the defendant acts for the purposes of sexual gratification, making answer A incorrect. The offence only applies to the genitals, not the buttocks, so the act of 'mooning' will not be covered, making answer B incorrect. A woman who exposes her breasts will not be guilty of an offence under s. 66, making answer D incorrect. If the genitals are not exposed for the relevant reason, the offence is not committed (correct answer C).

   Crime, para. 1.12.18.1

9. Answer **C** — The Criminal Law Act 1967, s. 3(1) states:

   A person may use such force as is reasonable in the circumstances in the prevention of crime or in effecting or assisting in the lawful arrest of offenders or suspected offenders or of persons unlawfully at large.

   So the starting point is to say that the use of '*reasonable* force' in self-defence or the defence of another is acceptable.

   Section 76 of the Criminal Justice and Immigration Act 2008 applies to s. 3(1) of the Criminal Law Act 1967, particularly to the question as to whether the degree of force used was reasonable in the circumstances. The 'degree of force' means the type and amount of force used. Section 76(10)(b) states that reasonable force in self-defence includes acting in the defence of another person. Answer B is incorrect as using force to defend another (MINCHER's wife) is acceptable—the issue now becomes whether the degree of force used was acceptable.

The question whether the degree of force used by the defendant was reasonable in the circumstances is to be decided by reference to the circumstances *as the defendant believed them to be* (s. 76(3)). Section 76(6) adds that the degree of force used by the defendant is not to be regarded as reasonable in the circumstances as the defendant believed them to be if it was *disproportionate* in those circumstances.

At this stage, it might appear that the force used by MINCHER was unacceptable if it were considered 'disproportionate' but s. 43 of the Crime and Courts Act 2013 amends s. 76 of the Criminal Justice and Immigration Act 2008 so that the use of *disproportionate* force can be regarded as reasonable in the circumstances as the accused believed them to be when *householders* are acting to protect themselves or others from trespassers in their homes (self-defence)—meaning that answer D is incorrect and that answer C is correct. The use of *grossly* disproportionate force would still not be permitted (making answer A incorrect).

Crime, paras 1.4.5.2 to 1.4.5.4

10. Answer **A** — 'Possession' requires custody or control and knowledge of possession. In relation to the cannabis in the bag and the khat, RAFFIN certainly has 'possession' of the items. However, he does not have possession of the cannabis seeds ordered by post—he would only have possession of the seeds ordered by post from the time they arrived through his letterbox (*R* v *Peaston* (1979) 69 Cr App R 203). This excludes options C and D as the correct answers. The other reason they are incorrect is that it is not an offence to possess cannabis seeds (they are not included in the definition of 'cannabis' under s. 37 of the Misuse of Drugs Act 1971). Cannabis resin is a Class B drug and khat is a Class C drug (meaning answer A is correct and answer B is incorrect).

Crime, paras 1.6.2 to 1.6.3.2

11. Answer **C** — The Theft Act 1968, s. 10(1) states that a person is guilty of aggravated burglary if they commit any burglary and at the time has with them any firearm or imitation firearm, any weapon of offence or any explosive (the 'classic' WIFE mnemonic—**W**eapon of Offence, **I**mitation Firearm, **F**irearm or **E**xplosive). What is required in the first place is a burglary (s. 9(1)(a) or (b)) to become aggravated. When WEBB breaks in intending to steal, a s. 9(1)(a) burglary is committed but at the time of committing it he does not have a WIFE item with him. In the office, there is only one burglary he can complete—a s. 9(1)(b) (steal or commit GBH/wounding or attempt to do either). When he is disturbed by the security guards and picks up the letter opener, he 'instantly' turns it into a weapon of offence but as he does not intend to steal it there is no s. 9(1)(a) burglary at this time. Threatening the security guards would not provide the circumstances of a s. 9(1)(b) and answer B is incorrect. Throwing the knife intending to cause serious injury to GEORGE is attempt GBH and is a s. 9(1)(b)—this is aggravated burglary so the correct answer is C. Aggravated burglary is committed when he injures PEACH but the question asks when the offence is *first* committed.

Crime, paras 1.14.5 to 1.14.6.1

12. Answer **A** — Answer B is incorrect as you cannot attempt to commit a summary only offence and a s. 39 assault/battery is a summary only offence. Answer C is incorrect as LOVE did not intend to cause grievous bodily harm to any person. Answer D is incorrect as the state of mind required for one offence can, on occasions, be 'transferred' from the

original target or victim to another. *This only operates if the crime remains the same*. In other words, a defendant cannot be convicted if he/she acted with the *mens rea* for one offence but commits the *actus reus* of another offence. In *R* v *Latimer* (1886) 17 QBD 359, the defendant lashed out with his belt at one person but missed, striking a third party instead. As it was proved that the defendant had the required *mens rea* when he swung the belt, the court held that the same *mens rea* could support a charge of wounding against any other victim injured by the same act. If the *nature of the offence* changes, then this approach will not operate. Therefore if a defendant is shown to have thrown a rock at a crowd of people intending to injure one of them, the *mens rea* required for that offence cannot be 'transferred' to an offence of criminal damage if the rock misses that person and breaks a window instead (*R* v *Pembliton* (1874) LR 2 CCR 119). The state of mind required for an offence under s. 20 of the Offences Against the Person Act 1861 is 'maliciousness' (recklessness) that 'some harm' will befall someone—that is exactly what has occurred here so LOVE is liable for the s. 20 offence against CLARKE. No contact is required for an assault at a s. 39 level—just the apprehension of immediate unlawful violence (correct answer A).

Crime, paras 1.1.11, 1.3.4, 1.10.7 to 1.10.7.3

13. Answer **B** — The Theft Act 1968, s. 17 states:

(1) Where a person dishonestly, with a view to gain for himself or another or with intent to cause loss to another,—
  (a) destroys, defaces, conceals or falsifies any account or any record or document made or required for any accounting purpose; or
  (b) in furnishing information for any purpose produces or makes use of any account, or any such record or document as aforesaid, which to his knowledge is or may be misleading, false or deceptive in a material particular;

he shall [commit an offence].

Answer A is incorrect as this is an 'intention' offence and no result is required—the fact that there was actually no loss or gain is immaterial. Answer C is incorrect as the offence can be committed in a number of ways which would include falsification of an account etc. and also omissions. Answer D is incorrect as there is no requirement to prove an intention permanently to deprive. Answer B is correct as an application for a mortgage or a loan to a commercial institution is a document required for an accounting purpose, the rationale being that applications for a mortgage or a loan to commercial institutions will, if successful, lead to the opening of an account which will show as credits in favour of the borrower any funds received from the borrower and will show as debits paid out by the lender to, or on behalf of, the borrower (*R* v *O and H* [2010] EWCA Crim 2233).

Crime, para. 1.15.10

14. Answer **C** — Recklessness is a state of mind that is relevant to a large number of crimes and is essentially concerned with unjustified risk-taking. Answer B is wrong as following the case of *R* v *G and R* [2003] UKHL 50, the approach taken to the interpretation of the word 'reckless' is that it will be 'subjective' and does not involve a 'reasonable bystander' test (which would effectively make the test 'objective').

The requirements of subjective recklessness can be found in the case of *R* v *Cunningham* [1957] 2 QB 396 and are satisfied in situations where *the defendant* foresees the consequences of his/her actions as being probable or even possible. In *G*, the House of Lords held that a person acts recklessly with respect to:

- a circumstance when he/she is *aware* of a risk that it exists or will exist;
- a result when he/she is *aware* of the risk that it will occur;

and it is, in the circumstances known to him/her, *unreasonable* to take that risk.

To establish recklessness therefore requires consideration of the degree of risk that is actually foreseen by the defendant of which he/she is aware and whether it was reasonable. Answer D is incorrect as whilst the risk a defendant is aware of may be small, that does not automatically mean that it is reasonable to take that risk. Each situation will be decided on its own merits but whether the risk is reasonable or not will be decided by the court—not the defendant. What this does is to introduce an objective element into the recklessness equation but, even though that is the case, it must be stressed that recklessness is still subjective—the key question is whether the defendant was aware of the risk.

Depending on the crime, the nature of the risk the defendant needs to be aware of will change. For example, to commit an offence under s. 20 of the Offences Against the Person Act 1861 (wounding or inflicting grievous bodily harm (see *Crime*, chapter 1.10)), the defendant must unlawfully and recklessly wound or inflict grievous bodily harm on the victim. Here 'recklessness' means that the defendant was aware of the risk that *some harm* would befall the victim, making answer A incorrect and answer C correct.

Crime, paras 1.1.3 to 1.1.3.3

15. Answer **B** — Answer A is incorrect as the circumstances in which an offence is to be taken as committed against a person acting in the exercise of functions as an emergency worker include circumstances where the offence takes place at a time when the person is not at work but is carrying out functions which, if done in work time, would have been in the exercise of functions as an emergency worker. 'Emergency workers' include police officers and persons employed for the purposes of providing, or engaged to provide, NHS health service (HARRIS and INGLEBY are 'emergency workers') making answer C incorrect. Answer D is incorrect as the fact that the victim of the offence is an emergency worker is an aggravating factor when considering other offences under the Offences Against the Person Act 1861. This is the case for a number of offences, such as s. 20 (malicious wounding/GBH), s. 18 (wounding/GBH with intent) and s. 47 (assault occasioning actual bodily harm) (s. 2(3)). Where this is the case, the court must treat the fact that the offence was committed on an emergency worker as an aggravating factor (that is to say, a factor that increases the seriousness of the offence) and must state in open court that the offence is so aggravated (s. 2(2)). This means the correct answer is B.

Crime, para. 1.10.6.2

16. Answer **B** — The Criminal Justice and Police Act 2001 allows courts (in practice, the Crown Court) to impose travel restrictions on offenders convicted of drug trafficking offences. A 'drug trafficking offence' is defined by s. 34 of the Act and includes the production of a

controlled drug (s. 4(2)), the *supply of a controlled drug* (s. 4(3)) and the importation/exportation offences under s. 3 along with inciting a person to commit these offences under s. 19 of the Misuse of Drugs Act 1971. It also includes aiding, abetting, counselling or procuring these offences. However, in addition to the offence the person is sentenced in relation to, sentence itself is relevant—for a travel restriction order to be imposed, the court must determine that a sentence of *four years or more* is appropriate. It is under a *duty* to consider whether or not a travel restriction order would be appropriate (s. 33). As MATTHEWS was only sentenced to three years' imprisonment, the travel restriction order is not appropriate (correct answer B).

Crime, para. 1.6.14

17. Answer **A** — The Public Order Act 1986, s. 38 states:

(1) It is an offence for a person, with the intention—
 (a) of causing public alarm or anxiety, or
 (b) of causing injury to members of the public consuming or using the goods, or
 (c) of causing economic loss to any person by reason of the goods being shunned by members of the public, or
 (d) of causing economic loss to any person by reason of steps taken to avoid any such alarm or anxiety, injury or loss,

to contaminate or interfere with goods, or make it appear that goods have been contaminated or interfered with, or to place goods which have been contaminated or interfered with, or which appear to have been contaminated or interfered with in a place where goods of that description are consumed, used, sold or otherwise supplied.

(2) It is also an offence for a person, with any such intention as is mentioned in paragraph (a), (c) or (d) of subsection (1), to threaten that he or another will do, or to claim that he or another has done, any of the acts mentioned in that subsection.

(3) It is an offence for a person to be in possession of any of the following articles with a view to the commission of an offence under subsection (1)—
 (a) materials to be used for contaminating or interfering with goods or making it appear that goods have been contaminated or interfered with, or
 (b) goods which have been contaminated or interfered with, or which appear to have been contaminated or interfered with.

Section 38(3) would capture RENDER's activities when he purchases the needles in the craft shop (correct answer A). The fact that the actual contamination activity occurred at RENDER's home address is irrelevant and this would be an offence under s. 38(1) so answer B is incorrect. Answer C is incorrect as when RENDER places the apples in the computer games aisle an offence is committed under s. 38(1)—the reference to 'in a place' in s. 38(1) should not be interpreted restrictively and placing the apples in the computer games sections would be placing them '*in a place* where goods of that description are consumed, used, sold or otherwise supplied'. Answer D is incorrect as 'goods' includes 'natural' goods (e.g. fruit and vegetables) or 'manufactured' goods (e.g. shampoo or disinfectant)—contaminating 'manufactured' goods with the needles would be just as much an offence as contaminating the apples.

Crime, para. 1.16.7

18. Answer **A** — An offence can be racially or religiously aggravated under s. 28(1)(a) of the Act (a demonstration of hostility) or s. 28(1)(b) of the Act (motivated by hostility)—or both, of course. Section 28(5) states that a 'religious group' means a group of persons defined by reference to religious belief of *lack of religious belief*. This means that atheists are a 'religious group'. Attacking the men in the pub was therefore motivated by religious hostility. There are a number of offences that are covered by s. 28 of the Act and whilst assaults are relevant (offences under s. 39 of the Criminal Justice Act 1988 (PIGGOTT) and ss. 47 and 20 of the Offences Against the Person Act 1861 (SHERLOCK)), a s. 18 offence is not covered (excluding BLOWER). Therefore answer A is correct.

Crime, paras 1.9.2 to 1.9.3, 1.9.3.5, 1.9.3.7

19. Answer **A** — Under s. 44 of the Act, a person commits an offence if he/she does an act capable or encouraging or assisting in the commission of an offence and he/she intends to encourage or assist its commission. The initial approach to FLAVELL by SIMPSON is all that is required for the offence to be committed (correct answer A) and although the offence is committed when SIMPSON offers cocaine to FLAVELL, option B states that it is only at that point that the offence is complete when it is actually complete at A. No 'end result' is required in terms of the person being approached forming an intention to commit a crime or the offence being committed (making answers C and D incorrect).

Crime, para. 1.3.2

20. Answer **D** — The first point to make is that RIMMER has committed an offence under s. 4(1) of the Road Traffic Act 1988 (driving whilst unfit). Section 4 of the Act states that a person who, when driving or attempting to drive a mechanically propelled vehicle on a road or other public place, is unfit to drive through drink or drugs is guilty of an offence. DC HALL would be entitled to arrest RIMMER in these circumstances, meaning that answer A is incorrect. Breaking the arm of the officer is a serious injury amounting to grievous bodily harm (according to the CPS charging standards), meaning that answer B is incorrect. Although RIMMER did not intend to injure the officer in this way, this is still a s. 18 offence. Section 18 wounding/GBH is committed when a person *unlawfully and maliciously* by any means whatsoever wounds or causes any grievous bodily harm to any person with intent to do some grievous bodily harm to any person, *or with intent to resist or prevent the lawful apprehension or detainer of any person*. It is the latter element that would cover RIMMER's behaviour as this is a form of the s. 18 offence. In these circumstances, RIMMER has maliciously caused grievous bodily harm to the officer with intent to resist or prevent the lawful apprehension etc. of any person. Here 'maliciously' means that the person must be subjectively reckless in relation to a risk of harm—RIMMER realises there is a risk of harm so that element is satisfied. The activity was carried out with intent to resist arrest so this is a s. 18 offence, meaning that answer C is incorrect.

Crime, paras 1.10.6.3 to 1.10.6.5

21. Answer **A** — It seems that, apart from the offences of murder, attempted murder, treason and offences under the Misuse of Drugs Act 1971, the defence is available against any other charge (including hijacking, *R* v *Abdul-Hussain* [1999] Crim LR 570), making answers B and C incorrect. Answer D is incorrect as the defence of 'duress of circumstances' (necessity) is only available when the crime is committed in order to avoid death or serious injury—here JUDGE is not committing the crime to avoid that outcome (JUDGE is the victim of blackmail, of course, but

you are not being questioned on that offence or the possible outcomes that these circumstances would have in reality—the question is asking about duress of circumstances and nothing else).

Crime, para. 1.4.4

22. Answer **B** — The Fraud Act 2006, s. 7 states:

    (1) A person is guilty of an offence if he makes, adapts, supplies or offers to supply any article—
    (a) knowing that it is designed or adapted for use in the course of or in connection with fraud, or
    (b) intending it to be used to commit, or assist in the commission of, fraud.

    The offence is committed in a number of ways—one of which is making an offer to supply any article intending it to be used to commit, or assist in the commission of, fraud. Therefore the offence is committed (answers A and C are incorrect). Further, it is the 'offer to supply' that is relevant here so answer D is incorrect and answer B is correct.

Crime, para. 1.15.8

23. Answer **D** — In *R* v *Maginnis* [1987] AC 303, the House of Lords held that 'supply' involves more than a mere transfer of physical control of the item from one person to another but includes a further concept; namely, that of 'enabling the recipient to apply the thing handed over to purposes for which he desires or has a duty to apply it'. In other words, *the person to whom the drug is given must derive some benefit from being given the drug*. So the key to working out if there has been a 'supply' is to ask, 'Does being given the drug benefit the person to whom the drug has been given?' If the answer is 'yes', then the person *giving the drug* is 'supplying' it. In *R* v *Dempsey* (1986) 82 Cr App R 291, a registered drug addict (A) was in lawful possession of a drug. A asked his partner (B) to hold on to some of that drug while he went to administer the remainder of it to himself in a gents' toilet. Both A and B were arrested, A being subsequently charged with 'supplying' B with the drug. There is no 'supply' from A to B as when A gives the drug to B, B *does not benefit from* the action; B is simply holding on to the drug (although, of course, B would be in unlawful possession of the drug at that stage). If A had given the drug to B for B to use, there would be a 'supply' by A to B as B *is benefiting* from the action; B gets to use the drug. If B intends to give back the drug to A, then B would commit the offence of possession with intent to supply. In *R* v *Maginnis* [1987] AC 303, a drug trafficker (A) temporarily left drugs with B; B expected A to pick up the drugs the following day and was charged and convicted of possession with intent to supply. The same approach taken with *Dempsey* applies. In *Maginnis*, when A gives the drugs to B, B does not benefit from it and there is no 'supply' from A to B; if B returns the drugs to A, there is a 'supply' from B to A as A benefits from being given the drug (to sell or use). As B intends to return the drug to A, B is in possession with intent to supply. If the drug trafficker in *Maginnis* had given the custodian of the drug £50 as a reward for holding the drug, then there would have been a 'supply' from A to B as B would benefit from holding the drug (he has been paid £50, benefiting financially from being given the drug). So when GRAHAM gives the drugs to SULLIVAN, SULLIVAN 'benefits' because he is being paid £500 and GRAHAM 'supplies' SULLIVAN, ruling out answers A and B. When SULLIVAN returns the drugs to GRAHAM, GRAHAM 'benefits' because he can sell the drugs and SULLIVAN 'supplies' GRAHAM ruling out answer C and making D the correct answer.

Crime, para. 1.6.4

24. Answer **D** — Answer A is incorrect as police officers can be victims of these offences and are entitled to the same protection under the legislation as anyone else (*R* v *Jacobs* [2001] 2 Cr App R (S) 38). Answer B is incorrect as a s. 39 offence can be racially or religiously aggravated. Answer C is incorrect as although the definition of a 'racist' incident is of critical importance to police officers, that definition ('a racist incident is any incident which is perceived to be racist by the victim or any other person') must not be confused with the definition of a 'racially or religiously aggravated' offence under s. 28 of the Crime and Disorder Act. A 'racist' incident does not automatically become a racially or religiously aggravated offence. As there has been a demonstration of racial (nationality) hostility based on the victim's membership or presumed membership of a racial group immediately before the s. 39 offence is carried out, the offence is committed (correct answer D).

Crime, paras 1.9.2 to 1.9.3.4

25. Answer **A** — Where a person is threatened with death or serious physical injury unless he/she carries out a criminal act, he/she may have a defence of duress (*R* v *Graham* [1982] 1 WLR 294). If defendants knowingly expose themselves to a risk of such a threat of death or serious physical injury, they cannot claim duress as a defence. So if a person joins a violent gang or an active terrorist organisation, he/she cannot claim duress as a defence to any crimes he/she may go on to commit under threat of death or serious injury from another member or rival of that organisation (*R* v *Sharp* [1987] QB 853). However, if the purpose of the organisation or gang is not predominantly violent or dangerous (e.g. a gang of shoplifters—or in this case burglars), the defence of duress *may* be available in relation to offences committed while under threat of death or serious physical injury from other gang members (*R* v *Shepherd* (1987) 86 Cr App R 47)—this eliminates option D. However, as the defence is not available in respect of an offence of murder (*R* v *Howe* [1987] AC 417) or attempted murder (*R* v *Gotts* [1992] 2 AC 412) as a principal or secondary offender, that eliminates options B and C leaving A as the correct answer.

Crime, para. 1.4.3

26. Answer **C** — A person commits an offence under s. 12 if, without having the consent of the owner or other lawful authority, he/she takes any conveyance for his/her own or another's use or, knowing that any conveyance has been taken without such authority, drives it or allows him/herself to be carried on it. The offence can be committed anywhere, making answer A incorrect. The conveyance must 'convey' you or another because you are in it or on it (or you intend for you or another to use it that way in the future). In this case, ASSENZA *pushes* the car 15 feet—it does not convey him, so he does not commit the offence. This makes answers B and D incorrect. Answer D is further incorrect as the 'lawful authority' element of the offence is not restricted in the way option D suggests; those individuals are mentioned in the *Crime Manual* but only as examples of who might have such lawful authority and not as a definitive list.

Crime, para. 1.14.7

27. Answer **B** — It is an offence at common law to take or carry away another person without the consent of that person and without lawful excuse. The required elements of this offence are the unlawful taking or carrying away of one person by another by force or *fraud* (*R* v *D* [1984] AC 778) (answer D is incorrect). The taking or carrying away of the victim must be without the

consent of the victim. If the victim consents to an initial taking but later withdraws that consent, the offence would be complete. If the consent is obtained by fraud, the defendant cannot rely on that consent and the offence will be made out (*R* v *Cort* [2003] EWCA Crim 2149). When SMITH is duped into attending the house by GRAY, she has certainly been subject to a fraud but there is no kidnap at this moment in time. That is because of the case law decision in *R* v *Hendy-Freegard* [2007] EWCA Crim 1236. In that case, the defendant was a confidence trickster who pretended to be an undercover agent working for MI5 or Scotland Yard. He told his victims that he was investigating the activities of the IRA and that his investigations had revealed that they were in danger. This allowed him to take control of their lives for years and, in doing so, to direct them to move about the country from location to location. The defendant was eventually arrested and convicted of kidnapping on the basis that the offence of kidnapping had occurred as his victims had made journeys around the country which they had been induced to make as a result of the defendant's false story. The defendant successfully appealed against the kidnapping conviction, with the court stating that causing a person to move from place to place when *unaccompanied by the defendant* could not itself constitute either taking or carrying away or deprivation of liberty, which were necessary elements of the offence. The offence is not committed when SMITH is duped to attend the house and answer A is incorrect. However, once at the location there is a fraud (GRAY is lying to SMITH) and he accompanies her into the house—the offence is complete at this point (correct answer B) which makes answer C incorrect.

Crime, para. 1.11.3

28. Answer **B** — Although triable either way, if the value of the property destroyed or the damage done is less than £5,000, the offence is to be tried summarily (Magistrates' Courts Act 1980, s. 22). However, if the damage in such a case was caused by fire (arson), this rule will not apply, making answer A incorrect. Arson (criminal damage by fire) is triable either way (not on indictment only) so answer C is incorrect.

Answer B is correct as the Theft Act 1968 states that where the property in question belonged to D's spouse or civil partner, a prosecution for unlawful damage may only be instituted against D by or with the consent of the DPP (s. 30(4)) (not the Attorney General—incorrect answer D).

Crime, para. 1.16.2

29. Answer **C** — A common assault by battery (beating) involves the actual use of force by an assailant on a victim but which only results in very minor or no perceivable injury. It is the intentional or reckless application of force on another and can range from a push to a punch, and depends on how much harm is done and the injury received. The application of force can be carried out indirectly—the circumstances of the question are such an example where injury is caused to the baby by SIMIC pulling back WALKER's hair and causing her to drop the baby to the ground causing slight injury. This is a s. 39 offence (a battery) meaning that answers B and D are eliminated. The offence under s. 47 of the Offences Against the Person Act 1861 (actual bodily harm (ABH)) is exactly the same as a s. 39 offence but can be distinguished from s. 39 by the degree of injury. It was held in *DPP* v *Smith (Ross Michael)* [2006] EWHC 94 (Admin) that the substantial cutting of a person's hair against his/her will could amount to actual bodily harm even though no pain or other injury may be involved. In *Smith*, the defendant cut off his ex-partner's ponytail, deliberately and without her permission. Even

though, medically and scientifically speaking, the hair above the surface of the scalp is no more than dead tissue, it remains part of the body and is attached to it. While it is so attached, it falls within the meaning of 'bodily' in the phrase 'actual bodily harm' as it is concerned with the body of the individual victim (answer A is incorrect). In this scenario, you have a s. 39 against the baby and a s. 47 committed against WALKER (correct answer C).

Crime, paras 1.10.6.1, 1.10.6.3, 1.10.7.3

30. Answer **A** — Under s. 3 of the Sexual Offences Act 2003, a person commits an offence if he/she intentionally touches another person (B), the touching is sexual, B does not consent to the touching and A does not reasonably believe that B consents. It does not have to involve touching the genitals (answer B is incorrect). 'Touching' includes (but is not limited to) touching with any part of the body (answer D is incorrect), with anything else or through anything else (e.g. clothing). The offence does not require that the activity is carried out for sexual gratification (answer C is incorrect).

Crime, paras 1.12.4.2 to 1.12.4.4

31. Answer **C** — Section 5(4) of the Theft Act 1968 states that where a person gets property by another's mistake and is under an obligation to make restoration (in whole or in part) of the property or its proceeds or of the value thereof then, to the extent of that obligation, the property or proceeds shall be regarded (as against him/her) as belonging to the person entitled to restoration, and an intention not to make restoration shall be regarded accordingly as an intention to deprive that person of the property or proceeds. Where extra money is mistakenly credited into an employee's bank account, the employee will be liable for stealing the extra money if he/she dishonestly keeps it (*Attorney-General's Reference (No. 1 of 1983)* [1985] QB 182 where a police officer's account was credited with money representing overtime which she had not actually worked). This clearly makes BAINES guilty of an offence of theft and makes answers B and D incorrect. Section 5(4) only applies where someone *other than the defendant* has made a mistake and as OLIVER mistakenly paid himself, s. 5(4) would not apply to him. But that does not mean he has not committed theft—if it did, then keeping property you obtain by your own error would not amount to theft (a bizarre scenario that would cause chaos in real life!). OLIVER would be caught by s. 3 of the Act which states (in relation to appropriation) that any assumption by a person of the rights of an owner amounts to an appropriation, and this includes, where he/she has come by the property (innocently or not) without stealing it, *any later assumption of a right to it by keeping or dealing with it as owner*. If you accidentally walked out of a shop with a bar of chocolate you meant to pay for but did not and then decided to keep it, you would be dishonest and guilty of theft—this is the same for OLIVER who accidentally walked out of the factory with an extra £50 and then decided to keep it (answer C is correct—answer A is incorrect).

Crime, paras 1.14.2.3, 1.14.2.8

32. Answer **D** — Unlike the other Fraud Act 2006 offences, the offence under s. 11 is not a conduct crime; it is a result crime and requires the actual obtaining of the service (answer A is incorrect). However, the offence does not require a fraudulent representation or deception (answer B is incorrect). Someone would commit this offence if, intending to avoid payment, he/she slipped into a concert hall to watch a concert without paying for the privilege. The

offence can be committed where the defendant intends to avoid payment or payment in full but the defendant must know that the services are made available on the basis that they are chargeable, i.e. services provided for free are not covered by the offence.

If D sneaks aboard a lorry or a freight train and obtains a free ride, D would commit no offence under s. 11 because the haulage company or freight train operator does not provide such rides, even for payment (correct answer D—this also makes answer C incorrect).

Crime, para. 1.15.9

33. Answer **D** — A principal offender is one whose conduct has met all the requirements of the particular offence (LEDDY). An accessory is someone who helped in or brought about the commission of the offence (COOPER and MARR). Answer B is incorrect as if an accessory 'aids, abets, counsels or procures' the commission of an offence, he/she will be treated by a court in the same way as a principal offender for an indictable offence (Accessories and Abettors Act 1861, s. 8) or for a summary offence (Magistrates' Courts Act 1980, s. 44). The expression 'aid, abet, counsel and procure' is generally used in its entirety when charging a defendant, without separating out the particular element that applies. Generally speaking, the expressions mean as follows:

- aiding = giving help, support or assistance (COOPER);
- abetting = inciting, instigating or encouraging.

Each of these would usually involve the presence of the secondary party at the scene (unless, for example, part of some pre-arranged plan):

- counselling = advising or instructing (MARR);
- procuring = bringing about.

So, COOPER and MARR are accessories (answer C is incorrect). Answer A is incorrect as if the principal cannot be traced or identified, the accessory may still be liable (*Hui Chi-Ming* v *The Queen* [1992] 1 AC 34).

As COOPER and MARR are accessories and will be treated in the same way as LEDDY, answer D is correct.

Crime, para. 1.2.8

34. Answer **D** — The Sexual Offences Act 2003, s. 51A (as amended) states:

(1) It is an offence for a person in a street or public place to solicit another (B) for the purpose of obtaining B's sexual services as a prostitute.
(2) The reference to a person in a street or public place includes a person in a vehicle in a street or public place.

The person solicited does not have to be a prostitute (incorrect answer A). Kerb-crawling or soliciting is punishable on the *first occasion* the activity takes place (correct answer D and making B incorrect in the process). In the case of kerb-crawling, there is no requirement for the soliciting to be shown to be likely to cause nuisance or annoyance to others (answer C is incorrect).

Crime, para. 1.12.15.5

35. Answer **C** — Section 25(1) of the Theft Act 1968 states that a person shall be guilty of an offence of going equipped if, when not at their place of abode, they have with them any article for use in the course of or in connection with any burglary or theft. Offences of fraud are not included within this definition (possession or control of such articles is subject to a separate offence under s. 6 of the Fraud Act 2006), meaning answer D is incorrect. The offence is directed against acts preparatory to the offences of burglary (contrary to s. 9 of the Theft Act 1968), theft (contrary to s. 1 of the Theft Act 1968) and taking a conveyance (contrary to s. 12 of the Theft Act 1968). 'Theft' includes theft with force which would amount to robbery, meaning that answer A is incorrect. The offence is committed when the person is 'not at their place of abode'—in other words, when they are away from their home. RHODES does not live at the bar and the fact that this is not a public place does not change the fact that he has committed the offence. In relation to 'have with him', it would suffice if defendants had the article within their immediate control in their car or bag, at their workplace or on their person, making answer B incorrect. As robbery is covered by the offence, the correct answer is C.

Crime, para. 1.14.10

36. Answer **A** — The Criminal Law Act 1977, s. 1 states:

(1) Subject to the following provisions of this Part of this Act, if a person agrees with any other person or persons that a course of conduct shall be pursued which, if the agreement is carried out in accordance with their intentions, either—
   (a) will necessarily amount to or involve the commission of any offence or offences by one or more of the parties to the agreement; or
   (b) would do so but for the existence of facts which render the commission of the offence or any of the offences impossible, he is guilty of conspiracy to commit the offence or offences in question.

Statutory conspiracy requires two or more persons (answer C is incorrect). Section 1(b) states that you can conspire to commit the 'impossible', so even though their intended victim is in hospital, this would not prevent a conspiracy to rape her (answer B is incorrect).'Dishonesty' is not part of the *mens rea* for this offence (answer D is incorrect). Answer A is correct as a defendant cannot be convicted of statutory conspiracy if the only other party to the agreement is:

- his/her spouse or civil partner;
- a person under the age of criminal responsibility, i.e. under 10 years of age;
- the intended victim (Criminal Law Act 1977, s. 2(2)).

Crime, para. 1.3.3.1

37. Answer **A** — Answers C and D are incorrect. In *R* v *B* [2006] EWCA Crim 2945, the Court of Appeal stated that whether an individual had a sexual disease or condition, such as being HIV-positive, was not an issue as far as consent was concerned. The case related to a man who was alleged to have raped a woman after they had met outside a nightclub. When arrested, the man informed the custody officer that he was HIV-positive, a fact he had not disclosed to the victim prior to sexual intercourse. At the original trial, the judge directed that this non-disclosure was relevant to the issue of consent. On appeal, the court stated that this was not the case and that the consent issue for a jury to consider was whether or not the victim consented to sexual

intercourse, not whether she consented to sexual intercourse with a person suffering from a sexually transmitted disease. However, in *R* v *McNally* [2013] EWCA Crim 1051 the Court of Appeal observed that *B* was not an authority that HIV status *could not* vitiate consent. *B* left the issue open and HIV status *could* vitiate consent if, for example, the complainant had been positively assured that the accused was not HIV-positive. However, in this MCQ such a positive assurance does not play any part in the scenario—RICHARDSON never mentioned his HIV status and the fact that he wore a condom does not have any impact in relation to this set of circumstances when considering the offence of rape; he would not commit that offence. However, the courts have recognised that person-to-person transmission of a sexual infection that will have serious consequences for the infected person's health can amount to grievous bodily harm under the Offences Against the Person Act 1861 (in *R* v *Dica* [2004] EWCA Crim 1103 there was an acceptance that the *deliberate* infection of another with the HIV virus could amount to grievous bodily harm). This issue was explored further in *R* v *Konzani* [2005] EWCA Crim 706. In that case, the defendant appealed against convictions for inflicting grievous bodily harm on three women contrary to s. 20. The defendant had unprotected consensual sexual intercourse with the women but *without having disclosed* that he was HIV-positive. The women subsequently contracted the HIV virus. The Court of Appeal held that there was a critical distinction between taking a risk as to the various potentially adverse (and possibly problematic) consequences of unprotected consensual intercourse and the giving of informed consent to the risk of infection with a fatal disease. Answer D is incorrect as the circumstances of this MCQ mean that RICHARDSON would commit a s. 20 offence (correct answer A).

Crime, paras 1.10.6.4, 1.12.3 to 1.12.3.1

38. Answer **B** — The Firearms Act 1968, s. 19 states:

A person commits an offence if, without lawful authority or reasonable excuse (the proof whereof lies on him), he has with him in a public place—

(a) a loaded shot gun,
(b) an air weapon (whether loaded or not),
(c) any other firearm (whether loaded or not) together with ammunition suitable for use in that firearm, or
(d) an imitation firearm.

An 'airsoft gun' is not to be regarded as a firearm for the purposes of this Act (s. 57A(1)). Section 57A(2) states that an 'airsoft gun' is a barrelled weapon of any description which:

- is designed to discharge only a small plastic missile (whether or not it is also capable of discharging any other kind of missile); and
- is not capable of discharging a missile (of any kind) with kinetic energy at the muzzle of the weapon that exceeds the permitted level.

A 'small plastic missile' is a missile made wholly or partly from plastics, is spherical and does not exceed 8 mm in diameter (s. 57A(3)).

The exemption is not absolute—if the kinetic energy at the muzzle exceeds the permitted level, then it will be a firearm. The 'permitted kinetic energy level' is:

- in the case of a weapon which is capable of discharging two or more missiles successively without repeated pressure on the trigger (an automatic weapon), 1.3 joules;
- in any other case (a single shot variant), 2.5 joules.

As the airsoft gun is a single shot variant with a kinetic energy level of 1.34 joules, it is not a firearm and possession of it is not an offence which makes answer A incorrect. Answer C is incorrect as the definition of a firearm under s. 57(1) of the Firearms Act 1968 does not include telescopic sights or magazines. Answer D is incorrect as a 'public place' includes any highway and any other premises or place to which, at the material time, the public have or are permitted to have access whether on payment or otherwise (s. 57(4) of the Act)—that would certainly include the showground WHARTON was searched in.

Crime, paras 1.7.2, 1.7.10.1

39. Answer **B** — Section 27 of the Theft Act 1968 allows for the admissibility of previous misconduct and states:

(3) Where a person is being proceeded against for handling stolen goods (but not for any offence other than handling stolen goods), then at any stage of the proceedings, if evidence has been given of his having or arranging to have in his possession the goods the subject of the charge, or of his undertaking or assisting in, or arranging to undertake or assist in, their retention, removal, disposal or realisation, the following evidence shall be admissible for the purpose of proving that he knew or believed the goods to be stolen goods—
(a) evidence that he has had in his possession, or has undertaken or assisted in the retention, removal, disposal or realisation of, stolen goods from any theft taking place not earlier than 12 months before the offence charged; and
(b) (provided that seven days' notice in writing has been given to him of the intention to prove the conviction) evidence that he has within the five years preceding the date of the offence charged been convicted of theft or of handling stolen goods.

When considering conviction under s. 27(3)(b), the relevant offences are theft or handling stolen goods (making answer A incorrect). The provisions under s. 27(3)(a) and (b) are *separate*—for example, evidence could be introduced regarding a defendant's conviction for theft three years preceding the offence charged (under s. 27(3)(b)). There is no need for the element under s. 27(3)(a) to be present *as well as* that theft conviction, making answer D incorrect. Both convictions could be introduced as evidence making answer C incorrect and answer B correct.

Crime, para. 1.14.11.4

40. Answer **C** — The Firearms Act 1968, s. 3 states:

(1) A person commits an offence if, *by way of trade or business*, he—
(a) manufactures, sells, transfers, repairs, tests or proves any firearm or ammunition to which section 1 of this Act applies, *or a shot gun*;
(b) exposes for sale or transfer, or has in his possession for sale, transfer, repair, test or proof any such firearm or ammunition, or a shot gun, or
(c) sells or transfers an air weapon, exposes such a weapon for sale or transfer or has such a weapon in his possession for sale or transfer,
without being registered under this Act as a firearms dealer.

The offence applies to shotguns (answer B is incorrect) and covers a wide variety of activities (not just 'sale or transfer') meaning answer D is incorrect. Answer A is incorrect as if the repair and service were carried out for free rather than by way of trade or business, then LUCY would commit an offence under s. 3(3) of the Act.

Crime, para. 1.7.5

41. Answer **C** — The Sexual Offences Act 2003, s. 47 states:

(1) A person (A) commits an offence if—
- (a) he intentionally obtains for himself the sexual services of another person (B),
- (b) before obtaining those services, he has made or promised payment for those services to B or a third person, or knows that another person has made or promised such a payment, and
- (c) either—
  - (i) B is under 18, and A does not reasonably believe that B is 18 or over, or
  - (ii) B is under 13.

The fact that PICKERING believes he is having sexual contact with a person who is 16 does not, in itself, make him guilty of a crime (answer A is incorrect). But PICKERING does commit the offence (answers B (the relevant age is 18) and D (sexual intercourse is not a requirement of the offence) are incorrect) as PICKERING's activities fill all the requirements of the offence (he has obtained the sexual services of HAZEL who is under 18 and he does not reasonably believe her to be 18 or over—correct answer C).

Crime, para. 1.12.11.1

42. Answer **B** — Section 1 of the Firearms Act 1968, s. 1 states:

(1) Subject to any exemption under this Act, it is an offence for a person—
- (a) to have in his possession, or to purchase or acquire, a firearm to which this section applies without holding a firearm certificate in force at the time, or otherwise than as authorised by such a certificate;
- (b) to have in his possession, or to purchase or acquire, any ammunition to which this section applies without holding a firearm certificate in force at the time, or otherwise than as authorised by such a certificate, or in quantities in excess of those so authorised.

So it is an offence to possess s. 1 ammunition without a certificate (making answer C incorrect) and that is the case regardless of the age of the person concerned (making answer A incorrect). Section 1 ammunition includes any ammunition for a firearm except:

- cartridges containing five or more shot, none of which is bigger than 0.36 inches in diameter;
- ammunition for an airgun, air rifle or air pistol; and
- blank cartridges not more than one inch in diameter (s. 1(4)).

The bullet is s. 1 ammunition—the cartridge containing ten shot is not—answer D is incorrect (the correct answer is B).

Crime, paras 1.7.4 to 1.7.4.2

43. Answer **A** — The defence of duress is not available in respect of an offence of murder (*R* v *Howe* [1987] AC 417). Answer C is incorrect as the threat can be made to 'loved ones'. Answer B is incorrect as although the threat drove CANNING to commit the offence, that is just one of the requirements and answer A supersedes this. Answer D is not correct as the requirement relating to time (imminently) relates to the threatened injury to the defendant or his/her 'loved ones'.

Crime, para. 1.4.3

44. Answer **C** — The Child Abduction Act 1984, s. 1 states:

(1) Subject to subsections (5) and (8) below, a person connected with a child under the age of 16 commits an offence if he takes or sends the child out of the United Kingdom without the appropriate consent.

Section 1(2) lists the people who are 'connected' with a child and that includes (at s. 1(2)(ca)) the 'special guardian of a child—so PLUCINSKI is connected to Gemma STAPLEY. Section 1(3) lists people who the 'appropriate consent' would be required from and that includes (at s. 1(3)(i)) the child's mother (Jane STAPLEY).

At this point, it seems that an offence has been committed but that is not the case (answers B and D are incorrect) as s. 1(4) of the Act states (*emphasis added*):

(4) A person ***does not commit an offence*** under this section by taking or sending a child out of the United Kingdom without obtaining the appropriate consent if—
   (a) he is a person named in a child arrangements order as a person with whom the child is to live, and he takes or sends the child out of the United Kingdom for a period of less than one month; or
   (b) ***he is a special guardian of the child and he takes or sends the child out of the United Kingdom for a period of less than three months***.

As PLUCINSKI is the special guardian of Gemma STAPLEY and he has not taken or sent her out of the United Kingdom for a period of three months or more, he does not commit the offence (correct answer C, making answer A incorrect (there is a time limit on how long the child can be taken/sent out of the United Kingdom)).

Crime, paras 1.13.2 to 1.13.2.2

45. Answer **A** — The Theft Act 1968, s. 9 states:

(1) A person is guilty of burglary if—
   (a) he enters any building or part of a building as a trespasser and with intent to commit any such offence as is mentioned in subsection (2) below; or . . .
(2) The offences referred to in subsection (1)(a) above are offences of stealing anything in the building or part of a building in question, of inflicting on any person therein any grievous bodily harm and of doing unlawful damage to the building or anything therein.

This means that HEWSON commits a s. 9(1)(a) burglary when he breaks in intending to commit criminal damage (correct answer A). Answers B and D are incorrect as s. 9(1)(b) burglary is committed by a person if, having entered any building or part of a building as a trespasser, they steal or attempt to steal anything in the building or that part of it or inflict or attempt to inflict on any person therein any grievous bodily harm (rape and damage for no part of the s. 9(1)(b) offence). Answer C is incorrect as a burglary is not committed when GILCHRIST's wife is raped.

Crime, paras 1.14.5 to 1.14.6.1

46. Answer **C** — Possession of cannabis or khat can be dealt with under the Penalty Notice for Disorder (PND) Scheme (answer A is incorrect). PNDs cannot be issued for any other drug-related offences other than possession of cannabis or cannabis derivatives (answer D is incorrect). PNDs may be issued to any adult found in possession of cannabis for personal use; they are not appropriate for offenders under the age of 18 (answer B is incorrect and answer C is the correct answer).

Crime, para. 1.6.3.7

47. Answer **B** — Section 21 of the Theft Act 1968 states:

(1) A person is guilty of blackmail if, with a view to gain for himself or another or with intent to cause loss to another, he makes any unwarranted demand with menaces; and for this purpose a demand with menaces is unwarranted unless the person making it does so in the belief—
  (a) that he has reasonable grounds for making the demand; and
  (b) that the use of the menaces is a proper means of reinforcing the demand.

There is no 'dishonesty' element in blackmail, making answer A incorrect (this actually relates to s. 2(1) of the Theft Act). Nor is there a requirement that the menace has a 'then and there' element to it (this is part of the definition of robbery under s. 8 of the Act), so answer C is incorrect. A blackmailer need not be seeking any kind of material profit. In *R* v *Bevans* (1988) 87 Cr App R 64, the defendant, who was crippled with arthritis, went to a doctor, produced a gun and demanded a pain-killing morphine injection, threatening to shoot the doctor if he did not comply; this was held to be blackmail as the drug involved was a form of property (answer D is incorrect). As all the elements of the offence are present, the correct answer is B.

Crime, paras 1.14.4 to 1.14.4.3

48. Answer **A** — The Criminal Attempts Act 1981, s. 1 states:

(1) If, with intent to commit an offence to which this section applies, a person does an act which is more than merely preparatory to the commission of the offence, he is guilty of attempting to commit the offence.
(2) A person may be guilty of attempting to commit an offence to which this section applies even though the facts are such that the commission of the offence is impossible.
(3) In any case where—
  (a) apart from this subsection a person's intention would not be regarded as having amounted to an intent to commit an offence; but
  (b) if the facts of the case had been as he believed them to be, his intention would be so regarded, then, for the purposes of subsection (1) above, he shall be regarded as having had an intent to commit that offence.

To prove an 'attempt', you must show an *intention* on the part of the defendant to commit the substantive offence. This requirement means that a higher level or degree of *mens rea* may be required to prove an attempt than for the substantive offence. For instance, the *mens rea* required to prove an offence of murder is the intention to kill *or* cause grievous bodily harm whereas the *mens rea* for attempted murder is nothing less than an *intent* to kill (*R* v *Whybrow* (1951) 35 Cr App R 141). FERGIE does not have the *mens rea* required to commit this offence (the intention to kill), making answer A correct and answers C and D incorrect. Answer B is incorrect as the fact that it would be impossible for FERGIE to throw acid over the pair would not preclude an attempted murder charge if he had the correct *mens rea*.

Crime, para. 1.3.4

49. Answer **A** — Under s. 3 of the Criminal Damage Act 1971:

A person who has anything in his custody or under his control intending without lawful excuse to use it or cause or permit another to use it:

(a) to destroy or damage any property belonging to some other person; or
(b) to destroy or damage his own or the user's property in a way which he knows is likely to endanger the life of some other person;
shall be guilty of an offence

The offence can take place anywhere, making answer B incorrect. Possession of the relevant article is one of the ways the offence can be committed; it can also be committed if a person has custody or control over the article. The correct answer is A as MAHON has custody of the shears as they are in her garden shed. The moment she decides to use them to commit criminal damage (custody + relevant intent), the offence is committed, making answers C and D incorrect.

Crime, para. 1.16.6

50. Answer **B** — The Children and Young Persons Act 1933, s. 1 states:

If any person who has attained the age of 16 years and has responsibility for any child or young person under that age, wilfully assaults, ill-treats (whether physically or otherwise), neglects, abandons, or exposes him, or causes or procures him to be assaulted, ill-treated (whether physically or otherwise), neglected, abandoned, or exposed, in a manner likely to cause him unnecessary suffering or injury to health (whether the suffering or injury is of a physical or a psychological nature), that person shall be guilty of an offence.

Assaulting Georgina and failing to feed Lorraine satisfy the *actus reus* of the offence; however, to commit the offence, the offender must be 16 or older (Caroline is 17 years old—this makes answer C incorrect) and the victim must be under 16 (this would exclude Georgina who is 16 years old and makes answer A incorrect). The offender must have 'responsibility' for the child. Responsibility for a child or young person can be shared and whether a person had such responsibility in each case will be a matter of both fact and law (*Liverpool Society for the Prevention of Cruelty to Children* v *Jones* [1914] 3 KB 813). Anyone having parental responsibility or any other legal liability to maintain a child or young person will be presumed to have responsibility for that child and that responsibility does not cease simply because the person ceases to have care of the child. Others such as babysitters may also have 'responsibility' for a child (answer D is incorrect). In this situation, the offence is committed by Caroline but only in respect of failing to feed Lorraine (correct answer B).

Crime, para. 1.13.3

51. Answer **D** — Section 8(1) of the Theft Act 1968 states that a person is guilty of robbery if he/she steals, and immediately before or at the time of doing so, and in order to do so, he/she uses force on any person or puts or seeks to put any person in fear of being then and there subjected to force. When BAYLEY threatens to urinate in LAW's car, you have an offence of blackmail but not robbery (making answer A incorrect). Robbery requires theft and at the stage where there is a threat to LAW's daughter there is not theft—once again, you have blackmail and answer B is consequently incorrect. A theft is committed when the £10 is handed over but that theft is associated with a threat of force—that threat is against LAW's daughter. This form of robbery requires the person to fear force for themselves—not for another—you cannot fear force for someone else and, once again, a blackmail is committed but no robbery (answer C is incorrect and answer D is correct).

Crime, para. 1.14.3

52. Answer **A** — Section 16 of the Offences Against the Person Act 1861 states that a person who without lawful excuse makes to another a threat, intending that that other would fear it would be carried out, to kill that other or a third person shall be guilty of an offence. This is all about the *intention of the person making the threat* (intending the other to believe) rather than other factors. So the fact that MEAD does not intend to follow through with the threat, or that ROWLAND does not believe MEAD or that the threat is to kill in the future are all immaterial and the offence has been committed (ruling out answers B, C and D and making answer A correct).

Crime, para. 1.10.8

53. Answer **A** — The offence of engaging in sexual activity in a public lavatory is committed when a person is in a lavatory to which the public or a section of the public has or is permitted to have access, whether on payment or otherwise (making answer B incorrect) and the person intentionally engages in an activity and that activity is sexual. Whether EVANS can be seen by anyone else is immaterial, making answer C incorrect. The activity does not have to take place with another, making answer D incorrect.

Crime, para. 1.12.18.4

54. Answer **C** — The Modern Slavery Act 2015, s. 12 states:

(1) If a person ('P') has been arrested for an offence under section 2, a constable or senior immigration officer may detain a relevant land vehicle, ship or aircraft.
(2) A land vehicle, ship or aircraft is relevant if the constable or officer has reasonable grounds to believe that an order for its forfeiture could be made under section 11 if P were convicted of the offence.
(3) The land vehicle, ship or aircraft may be detained—
  (a) until a decision is taken as to whether or not to charge P with the offence,
  (b) if P has been charged, until P is acquitted, the charge against P is dismissed or the proceedings are discontinued, or
  (c) if P has been charged and convicted, until the court decides whether or not to order forfeiture of the vehicle, ship or aircraft.

The power relates to land vehicles as well as ships and aircraft (making answer D incorrect). The vehicle could be detained in any of the circumstances under s. 12(3), meaning that answer

B is incorrect. An inspector does not have to authorise the use of the power (answer A is incorrect). As per s. 12(2), answer C is correct.

Crime, para. 1.11.4.2

55. Answer **B** — As an offence contrary to s. 5 of the 1968 Act is a strict liability offence, there is no need to prove that the accused knew the nature of the thing he/she possessed (that it was a firearm or ammunition) in order to prove the offence—it is sufficient to establish that the accused was in possession of the article (*R* v *Deyemi* [2007] EWCA Crim 2060). For example, in *Price* v *DPP* [1996] CLY 1469 an accused was held to have been in possession of the contents of a rucksack (ammunition) notwithstanding that he had no idea of its contents, and was indeed mistaken as to whom it belonged, and as to its nature and quality. If an accused is carrying a rucksack and the rucksack contains ammunition for a section 1 firearm, the accused is in 'possession' of the ammunition irrespective of his/her knowledge or ignorance of its presence in the rucksack (*R* v *Waller* [1991] Crim LR 381; *R* v *Cremin* [2007] EWCA Crim 666) (answer D is incorrect). This seems to make answer C correct but it is not as the washing-up bottle containing acid is not a prohibited weapon (correct answer B). The full list of prohibited weapons and ammunition is contained in s. 5(1) and (1A) of the Firearms Act 1968. This list often (but not always) relates to weapons used in a military context and includes any weapon, of whatever description, designed or adapted for the discharge of any noxious liquid, gas or other thing. However, in relation to weapons designed or adapted for the discharge of any noxious liquid, gas or other thing, taking an empty washing-up bottle and filling it with hydrochloric acid *does not* amount to adapting it, neither is such a thing a 'weapon' for the purposes of s. 5 (*R* v *Formosa*; *R* v *Upton* [1991] 2 QB 1). This is because to do so does not change the nature of the washing-up bottle itself as the bottle has not been adapted or altered and is therefore not a weapon 'designed or adapted' for the discharge of any noxious liquid etc. Answer A is wrong because it states that the offence is not committed as BLACK did not know the washing-up bottle containing acid was there—in other words, if he *did* know it was there the offence would be committed—*it would not*.

Crime, paras 1.7.7 to 1.7.7.2

56. Answer **C** — The Criminal Attempts Act 1981 tells us that an attempt is an action that is 'more than merely preparatory' to the commission of an offence. Buying the materials to make a petrol bomb and walking over to KENT's house are merely preparatory (answers A and B are incorrect). Liability comes about at point C where BARKER tries to commit the offence of arson (correct answer C and this makes answer D incorrect). The fact that the petrol bomb does not ignite is immaterial—if it did, this would amount to the substantive offence of arson.

Crime, para. 1.3.4

57. Answer **D** — The offence does not require communication on two or more occasions (answer A is incorrect). Answers B and C are incorrect as under s. 15A of the Sexual Offences Act 2003 it is an offence for a person aged 18 or over to communicate with a person under the age of 16 years if the communication is for the purpose of sexual gratification for the sender.

Crime, para. 1.12.7.8

58. Answer **C** — A person who without lawful excuse destroys or damages any property belonging to another intending to destroy or damage such property or being reckless as to whether any such property will be damaged or destroyed commits an offence of criminal damage (s. 1(1) of the Criminal Damage Act 1971). 'Property' includes money which makes answer B incorrect. The property must 'belong to another' and as the shirts belong to STARR (they were given to him as a gift), then he cannot commit the s. 1(1) offence in relation to them meaning that answer A is incorrect. However, it is possible for a person to commit criminal damage to his/her own property if it also belongs to someone else (e.g. the property in question is jointly owned). As the money belongs to STARR and to KIERNAN, then STARR can damage it, meaning that answer D is incorrect and answer C is correct.

Crime, paras 1.16.2 to 1.16.2.3

59. Answer **C** — There are a number of sch. 1 offences and they include an offence of child abduction under s. 1 of the Child Abduction Act 1968 (making answer B incorrect). The offence includes possession of an imitation firearm (making answer D incorrect). Answer A is incorrect as there is no need for the defendant to be subsequently *convicted* of the sch. 1 offence, or even to prove that it has been committed; all that is needed is to show that the defendant, at the time of the commission of the sch. 1 offence and/or of his/her arrest for a sch. 1 offence, had a firearm/imitation firearm in his/her possession (*R* v *Nelson* [2001] QB 55). The offence has been committed in these circumstances (correct answer C).

Crime, para. 1.7.9.5

60. Answer **C** — The Offences Against the Person Act 1861, s. 4 states:

Whosoever shall solicit, encourage, persuade or endeavour to persuade, or shall propose to any person, to murder any other person, whether he be a subject of Her Majesty or not, and whether he be within the Queen's dominions or not, shall be guilty of [an offence].

Although the soliciting must be done from within the jurisdiction, the phrase 'whether he be a subject of Her Majesty or not, and whether he be within the Queen's dominions or not' has been interpreted so that it applies not only to the person to be murdered but also to the person being solicited (for 'Queen' read 'King'—the legislation has not caught up with the change of monarch). Thus, in *R* v *Abu Hamza* [2007] QB 659, it was no defence that the persons being solicited were of various nationalities and the murders were to take place abroad and that it was not proved that any of those solicited to murder were British nationals. This means that answers B and D are incorrect.

The proposed victim may be outside the United Kingdom.

Answer A is incorrect as it does not matter whether or not the person is in fact encouraged to commit murder (correct answer is therefore C), but the offence is not complete until someone is in receipt of the solicitation, although the act of sending it can constitute an attempt (*R* v *Krause* (1902) 66 JP 121).

Crime, para. 1.5.7

61. Answer **B** — Where a person is arrested at any place other than a police station, or taken into custody by a constable following an arrest made by a civilian, the constable is normally obliged to take that person to a designated police station (Police and Criminal Evidence Act 1984 (PACE84), s. 30(1), (1A), (1B) and (2)), or in certain circumstances to a non-designated police station (s. 30(3) to (6)). An arrested person may, instead of being taken to a police station, be released with bail (known as 'street bail') or without bail to attend at a police station at a later date—this makes answer A incorrect. Answer C is incorrect as the fact that the offence of theft is an indictable offence does not impact on PC CHU's ability to grant 'street bail'. Section 30A(3B) enables the officer granting bail to consider attaching conditions relevant and proportionate to the suspect and the offence. The conditions that may be considered are the same as those available to a custody officer as contained in s. 3A(5) of the 1976 Act, except for those specified in s. 30A(3A)—this makes answer D incorrect. A custody officer must authorise the release on bail having considered any representations made by the person (s. 30(1A)(b)) and the correct answer at option B.

Evidence and Procedure, paras 2.2.2 to 2.2.2.1

62. Answer **A** — The Criminal Procedure Rules 2020, r. 4.3 states:

(1) A document may be served on—
  (a) an individual by handing it to him or her;
  (b) a corporation by handing it to a person holding a senior position in that corporation;
  (c) an individual or corporation who is legally represented in the case by handing it to that legal representative;
  (d) ...
  (e) ...
(2) If an individual is under 18, a copy of a document served under paragraph (1)(a) must be handed to his or her parent, or another appropriate adult, unless no such person is readily available.

The Criminal Procedure Rules 2020, r. 4.4 states:

(1) A document may be served by addressing it to the person to be served and leaving it at the appropriate address for service under this rule, or by sending it to that address by first class post or by the equivalent of first class post.
(2) The address for service under this rule on—
  (a) an individual is an address where it is reasonably believed that he or she will receive it;
  (b) a corporation is its principal office, and if there is no readily identifiable principal office then any place where it carries on its activities or business.

Answer A is correct as the documents could be served by handing them personally to RANKINE or FINLEY (making answers B and C incorrect). The documents can be served by post (answer D is incorrect).

Evidence and Procedure, para. 2.1.3

63. Answer **A** — Code E, para. 4.12(c) states that if the suspect fails to accept or to acknowledge receipt of the notice, the interviewer will state for the recording that a copy of the notice has been provided to the suspect and that he/she has refused to take a copy of the notice or has refused to acknowledge receipt (correct answer A).

Evidence and Procedure, para. 2.8.10

64. Answer **B** — The custody officer should record any comment the detainee makes in relation to the arresting officer's account, but shall not invite comment (Code C, para. 3.4); this makes answer C incorrect (and answer B correct, of course). The custody officer shall not put specific questions to the detainee regarding their involvement in any offence or in respect of any comments made in response to the arresting officer's account, making answers A and D incorrect.

Evidence and Procedure, para. 2.6.8

65. Answer **C** — Section 76A of PACE84 states that as long as it has not been excluded by the court under s. 76A (which makes similar provisions for exclusion as those under s. 76), in any proceedings where a confession was made by one accused person it may be given in evidence for another person charged in the same proceedings (a co-accused); answer D is therefore incorrect as the fact that the confession is from NELDER would not, in itself, be reason to rule the confession inadmissible. The key part of this subsection is that the co-accused must be 'charged in the same proceedings', for instance, in *R* v *Finch* [2007] EWCA Crim 36 where one suspect pleaded guilty the court held that he was no longer a person charged or accused in the trial, accordingly s. 76A of the 1984 Act did not apply and what he said to the police was not admissible (making answers A and B incorrect).

Evidence and Procedure, para. 2.4.2

66. Answer **C** — Annex A of Code C deals with intimate searches. Body orifices other than the mouth may be searched under s. 55(1) of PACE84 only if authorised by an officer of inspector rank or above who has reasonable grounds for believing that the person may have concealed on themselves:

(a) anything which they could and might use to cause physical injury to themselves or others at the station; or
(b) a Class A drug which they intended to supply to another or to export;
(c) and the officer has reasonable grounds for believing that an intimate search is the only means of removing those items.

A search authorised to locate a Class A drug may only be carried out by a registered medical practitioner or registered nurse (making answers A and D incorrect). Such a search can take place at a hospital, surgery or other medical premises (making answer B incorrect and answer C correct).

Evidence and Procedure, para. 2.6.22

67. Answer **D** — A non-intimate sample may be taken from a detainee in a variety of circumstances (see para. 6.6 of Code D). This applies whether or not the person is a juvenile, making answer A incorrect. Code D, para. 6.7 states that reasonable force may be used, if

necessary, to take a non-intimate sample from a person without their consent and does not require the authority of an inspector or above, making answer B incorrect. Code D, para. 6.10 states that a record will be made of the process and, if force is used, the record will include the circumstances and those present. Written consent does not have to be provided by the detainee, making answer C incorrect.

Evidence and Procedure, para. 2.7.7.2

68. Answer **D** — The Youth Justice and Criminal Evidence Act 1999 provides that both prosecution and defence witnesses are eligible for special measures, and the categories of eligibility include:

- all witnesses under the age of 18 at the time of the hearing or video recording (s. 16(1)(a));
- vulnerable witnesses who are affected by a mental disorder, impairment of intelligence and social functioning (s. 16(2)(a)(i), (ii));
- vulnerable witnesses who are affected by physical disability or disorder (s. 16(2)(b));
- witnesses in fear or distress about testifying (s. 17(1));
- any witness to a 'relevant offence', currently defined to include homicide offences and other offences involving a firearm or knife (s. 17(5)–(7), sch. 1A);
- adult victims of domestic violence who are vulnerable or intimidated;
- adult complainants of sexual offences (as defined by s. 62 of the 1999 Act), human trafficking offences (s. 59A of the Sexual Offences Act 2003 or s. 4 of the Asylum and Immigration (Treatment of Claimants, etc.) Act 2004), indecent photographs of children offences (s. 1 of the Protection of Children Act 1978 (take, permit to be taken or publish etc. such a photograph), s. 160 of the Criminal Justice Act 1988 (possession of such a photograph)), slavery and trafficking offences (ss. 1 and 2 of the Modern Slavery Act 2015) and an offence of domestic abuse under the Domestic Abuse Act 2021.

The eligibility criteria means that answer A is incorrect. In relation to the category 'any witness to a "relevant offence" involving a firearm, offensive weapon or knife', the 'relevant offence' is an offence specified in sch. 1A to the 1999 Act that includes murder, manslaughter, wounding, assault etc. All witnesses involved in such cases, including police officers, are automatically eligible for a special measures direction unless they decline (s. 17(5)); this means that answer B is incorrect. Answer C is incorrect as the primary rule is that all witnesses under the age of 18, regardless of the nature of the offence charged, are eligible for their evidence to be given by video interview and the use of live link; this does not prohibit a child witness who wishes to testify in court (ss. 21 and 22) (correct answer D).

Evidence and Procedure, para. 2.3.10.1

69. Answer **B** — Answer C is incorrect as para. 11.1 of Code C states that following a decision to arrest a suspect, they must not be interviewed about the relevant offence except at a police station or other authorised place of detention, unless the consequent delay would be likely to:

(a) lead to:
- interference with, or harm to, evidence connected with an offence;
- interference with, or physical harm to, other people; or
- serious loss of, or damage to, property;

(b) lead to alerting other people suspected of committing an offence but not yet arrested for it; or

(c) hinder the recovery of property obtained in consequence of the commission of an offence.

Answers A and D are incorrect as a juvenile can be interviewed without an appropriate adult being present if an officer of superintendent rank or above considers that delaying the interview will lead to the consequences in para. 11.1(a) to (c), and is satisfied that the interview would not significantly harm the person's physical or mental state.

Evidence and Procedure, para. 2.8.3

70. Answer **C** — Delivering a 'special warning' (under s. 36 or 37 of the Criminal Justice and Public Order Act 1994) does not hinge on whether the detained person is legally represented in interview or not—a person who is not legally represented can be given a 'special warning', making answer D incorrect. Section 37 is only concerned with the suspect's location *at the time of arrest* and applies only when he/she was found at that location at or about the time of the offence. It would not apply where the suspect has been seen near the scene of a crime but is arrested elsewhere (making answers A and B incorrect and answer C correct). In such circumstances, the provisions for mentioning relevant facts in s. 34 of the Act are likely to be appropriate. In addition, s. 38(3) states that an accused cannot be convicted solely on an inference drawn from a failure or refusal to answer questions, making answer B further incorrect) and, if given, the 'special warning' can be given by the interviewing constable (it does not have to be the officer who saw and arrested the person at the relevant locations (making answer A further incorrect)).

Evidence and Procedure, para. 2.8.2

71. Answer **A** — Section 125CA(3) of the Magistrates' Courts Act 1980 states that a disclosure order is an order requiring the person to whom it is directed to supply the designated officer for the court with any of the following information about the person to whom the warrant relates:

(a) his/her name, date of birth or national insurance number;
(b) his/her address (or any of his/her addresses).

This makes answer A correct and answers B, C and D incorrect.

Evidence and Procedure, para. 2.1.6.1

72. Answer **C** — Section 80(2A)(b) of PACE84 states that in any proceedings the spouse or civil partner of a person charged in the proceedings shall, subject to subs. (4), be compellable to give evidence for the prosecution but only in respect of any specified offence with which any person is charged in the proceedings. The Marriage (Same Sex Couples) Act 2013 extended marriage to same-sex couples and the Partnership (Opposite-sex Couples) Regulations 2019 extended civil partnership to opposite-sex couples so s. 80 is applicable to same-sex marriages and answer A is incorrect. Section 80(3) defines a 'specified offence' and that includes one that involves an assault on, or injury or a threat of injury to, the spouse or civil partner, making answer C correct (and answers B and D incorrect).

Evidence and Procedure, para. 2.3.8.5

73. Answer **B** — Paragraph 9.3 of Code C states that detainees should be visited at least every hour. If no reasonable risk was identified in a risk assessment, there is no need to wake a sleeping detainee (making answers C and D incorrect in relation to MUNDI). Those suspected of being intoxicated through drink or drugs or having swallowed drugs or whose level of

consciousness causes concern must, subject to any clinical direction given by an appropriate health-care professional, be visited and roused at least every half hour (making answer A incorrect).

Evidence and Procedure, para. 2.6.14

74. Answer **B** — PACE Code C, para. 12.5 states that a suspect whose detention without charge has been authorised under PACE84 because the detention is necessary for an interview to obtain evidence of the offence for which they have been arrested, may choose not to answer questions but the police do not require the suspect's consent or agreement to interview them for this purpose (answer A is incorrect). If a suspect takes steps to prevent themselves being questioned or further questioned, e.g. by refusing to leave their cell to go to a suitable interview room or by trying to leave the interview room, they shall be advised that their consent or agreement to interview is not required. The suspect shall be cautioned and informed that if they fail or refuse to cooperate, the interview may take place in the cell and that their failure or refusal to cooperate may be given in evidence. The suspect shall then be invited to cooperate and go into the interview room. If they refuse and the custody officer considers, on reasonable grounds, that the interview should not be delayed, the custody officer has discretion to direct that the interview be conducted in a cell (correct answer B—meaning answers C and D are incorrect).

Evidence and Procedure, para. 2.8.4

75. Answer **D** — The Bail Act 1976, s. 7 states:

(3) A person who has been released on bail in criminal proceedings and is under a duty to surrender into the custody of a court may be arrested without warrant by a constable—
   (a) if the constable has reasonable grounds for believing that person is not likely to surrender to custody;
   (b) if the constable has reasonable grounds for believing that that person is likely to break any of the conditions of his bail or has reasonable grounds for suspecting that that person has broken any of those conditions; or
   (c) in a case where that person was released on bail with one or more surety or sureties, if a surety notifies a constable in writing that that person is unlikely to surrender to custody and that for that reason the surety wishes to be relieved of his obligations as a surety.

So PC WINN was correct to arrest XIA (as per s. 7(3)(c)), making answer A incorrect. Answer B is incorrect as s. 7 does not create an offence, it merely confers a power of arrest (*R* v *Gangar* [2008] EWCA Crim 2987). Answer C is incorrect as where a person is arrested under s. 7, he/she shall be brought before a magistrate as soon as practicable and in any event within 24 hours (s. 7(4)(a))—correct answer D. However, in the case of a person charged with murder, or with murder and one or more other offences, he/she must be brought before a judge of the Crown Court (s. 7(8)). This section requires that a detainee not merely be brought to the court precincts or cells but actually be dealt with by a justice within 24 hours of being arrested (*R (On the application of Culley)* v *Dorchester Crown Court* [2007] EWHC 109 (Admin)).

Evidence and Procedure, para. 2.2.8

76. Answer **C** — Paragraph 3.25 of PACE Code E states that a police officer has no authority to break the seal on a master recording which is required for criminal trial or appeal proceedings. If it is necessary to gain access to the master recording, the police officer shall arrange for its seal to be broken in the presence of a representative of the Crown Prosecution Service. The defendant or their legal adviser should be informed and given a reasonable opportunity to be present. If the defendant or their legal representative is present, they shall be invited to re-seal and sign the master recording. If either refuses or neither is present, this should be done by the representative of the Crown Prosecution Service (answers A, B and D are incorrect—answer C is the correct answer).

Evidence and Procedure, para. 2.8.9

77. Answer **C** — A confession is defined by s. 82(1) of PACE84 as a 'statement wholly or partly adverse to the person who made it, whether made to a person in authority or not and whether made in words or otherwise'. This means that the response to the question asked by MASON and the statement to PC SIDHU would be confessions (answers A, B and D are incorrect).

Evidence and Procedure, para. 2.4.2

78. Answer **B** — In *Johnson*, Watkins LJ at pp. 1385–6 gave the following guidance as to the minimum evidential requirements needed if disclosure is to be protected:

    (a) The police officer in charge of the observations to be conducted, no one of lower rank than a sergeant, should usually be acceptable for this purpose, must be able to testify that beforehand he/she visited all observation places to be used and ascertained the attitude of the occupiers of premises, not only to the use to be made of them, but to the possible disclosure thereafter of the use made and facts which could lead to the identification of the premises thereafter and of the occupiers. He/she may, of course, in addition inform the court of difficulties, if any, usually encountered in the particular locality of obtaining assistance from the public.
    (b) A police officer of no lower rank than a chief inspector must be able to testify that immediately prior to the trial he/she visited the places used for observations, the results of which it is proposed to give in evidence, and ascertained whether the occupiers are the same as when the observations took place and, whether they are or are not, what the attitude of those occupiers is to the possible disclosure of the use previously made of the premises and of facts which could lead at the trial to identification of the premises and occupiers.

    Paragraph (a) means that answers A, C and D are incorrect.

Evidence and Procedure, para. 2.5.9.5

79. Answer **B** — Annex B of Code D (para. 9) states that an identification parade shall consist of at least eight people (in addition to the suspect) who, so far as possible, resemble the suspect in age, height, general appearance and position in life. Only one suspect shall be included in an identification parade *unless there are two suspects of roughly similar appearance, in which case they may be paraded together with at least 12 other people* (correct answer B). So the parade can take place (making answer A incorrect) and will be with at least 12 other people

(making answer D incorrect). There is no requirement for certification that such a procedure should take place because of expediency (answer C is incorrect).

Evidence and Procedure, para. 2.7.9

80. Answer **A** — The duty to retain material includes in particular the duty to retain certain material—that includes final versions of witness statements (and draft versions where their content differs from the final version)—correct answer A. It would extend to communications between the police and experts such as forensic scientists, reports of work carried out by experts and schedules of scientific material prepared by the expert for the investigator, for the purposes of criminal proceedings (making answer D incorrect). It does not extend to duplicate copies of records or reports (answer B is incorrect). Answer C is incorrect as in deciding what material should be retained in an investigation, consideration should be given to any force orders, what powers there are to seize and retain the said material as well as the Disclosure Code and the A-G's Guidelines. Where an investigator discovers material that is relevant to the case, he/she must record that information or retain the material (Code, para. 5.1).

Evidence and Procedure, paras 2.5.8 to 2.5.8.1

81. Answer **B** — Answer D is incorrect as s. 25(1) of the Criminal Justice and Public Order Act 1994 states that a person who in any proceedings has been charged with or convicted of an offence to which this section applies in circumstances to which it applies shall be granted bail in those proceedings only if the court or, as the case may be, *the constable* considering the grant of bail is of the opinion that there are *exceptional circumstances which justify it*. Section 25 provides that bail may not be granted where a person is charged with one of the offences below and also has a conviction for one of those offences:

(a) murder;
(b) attempted murder;
(c) manslaughter;
(d) rape under the law of Scotland;
(e) an offence under section 1 of the Sexual Offences Act 1956 (rape);
(f) an offence under section 1 of the Sexual Offences Act 2003 (rape);
(g) an offence under section 2 of that Act (assault by penetration);
(h) an offence under section 4 of that Act (causing a person to engage in sexual activity without consent) where the activity caused involved penetration within subsection (4)(a) to (d) of that section;
(i) an offence under section 5 of that Act (rape of a child under 13);
(j) an offence under section 6 of that Act (assault of a child under 13 by penetration);
(k) an offence under section 8 of that Act (causing or inciting a child under 13 to engage in sexual activity), where an activity involving penetration within subsection (3)(a) to (d) of that section was caused;
(l) an offence under section 30 of that Act (sexual activity with a person with a mental disorder impeding choice), where the touching involved penetration within subsection (3)(a) to (d) of that section;
(m) an offence under section 31 of that Act (causing or inciting a person, with a mental disorder impeding choice, to engage in sexual activity), where an activity involving penetration within subsection (3)(a) to (d) of that section was caused;

...

(n) an attempt to commit an offence within any of paragraphs (d) to (m).

As LUCAS has a conviction for assault by penetration (mentioned at s. 25(2)(g)) and is charged with an offence of sexual activity with a person with a mental disorder impeding choice that involves penetration (mentioned at s. 25(2)(l)), the provisions of s. 25 will be applicable—this eliminates answers A and C.

Evidence and Procedure, para. 2.2.5

82. Answer **C** — If MARSH refuses then an inspector can provide oral authorisation that he be examined, although this will have to be confirmed in writing as soon as practicable (Code D, para. 5.8). MARSH's consent is not required but if it is given then an inspector's authority is not required, making answer D incorrect. The power can be used to establish the identity of an individual or to identify them as a person involved in the commission of an offence, making answer A incorrect. Force can be used if necessary, making answer B incorrect.

Evidence and Procedure, para. 2.7.6

83. Answer **D** — The 'relevant time' of a person's detention starts in accordance with s. 41(2)–(5) of PACE84. The time from which the period of detention of a person is to be calculated (in this Act referred to as 'the relevant time') will be in the case of a person arrested outside England and Wales, the time at which that person arrives at the first police station to which he/she is taken in the police area in England or Wales in which the offence for which he/she was arrested is being investigated (17.30hrs Wednesday) or the time 24 hours after the time of that person's entry into England and Wales whichever is the earlier.

Evidence and Procedure, para. 2.6.17.1

84. Answer **A** — Code D, para. 3.11 states that no officer or any other person involved with the investigation of the case against the suspect may take any part in those procedures or act as the identification officer, meaning that answers C and D are incorrect. Paragraph 3.11 also states that arrangements for, and conduct of, the eye-witness identification procedures in paras 3.5 to 3.10 and circumstances in which any such identification procedure must be held shall be the responsibility of an officer not below inspector rank who is not involved with the investigation ('the identification officer'). This would appear to mean that answer B is correct; however, para. 3.19 states that in the case of a detained suspect, the duties under paras 3.17 and 3.18 (providing an explanation of the identification procedure and the notice in relation to it) may be performed by the custody officer or by another officer or police staff not involved in the investigation as directed by the custody officer, if:

(a) it is proposed to release the suspect in order that an identification procedure can be arranged and carried out and an inspector is not available to act as the identification officer, before the suspect leaves the station; or
(b) it is proposed to keep the suspect in police detention whilst the procedure is arranged and carried out and waiting for an inspector to act as the identification officer would cause unreasonable delay to the investigation.

The officer concerned shall inform the identification officer of the action taken and give them the signed copy of the notice. Therefore answer A is the correct option.

Evidence and Procedure, para. 2.7.4.2

85. Answer **D** — Where a person is remanded in custody, it normally means detention in prison. However, s. 128 of the Magistrates' Courts Act 1980 provides that a magistrates' court may remand a person to police custody:

- for a period not exceeding three clear days (24 hours for persons under 18 (s. 91(5) of the Legal Aid, Sentencing and Punishment of Offenders Act 2012) (s. 128(7)); this makes answers B and C incorrect;
- for the purpose of enquiries into offences (other than the offence for which he/she appears before the court) (s. 128(8)(a)); this makes answer A incorrect;
- as soon as the need ceases, he/she must be brought back before the magistrates (s. 128(8)(b));
- the conditions of detention and periodic review apply as if the person was arrested without warrant on suspicion of having committed an offence (s. 128(8)(c) and (d)) (correct answer D).

Evidence and Procedure, para. 2.2.10

86. Answer **B** — Section 55A of PACE84 allows a person who has been arrested and is in police detention to have an X-ray taken of them or an ultrasound scan to be carried out on them (or both) if:

(a) authorised by an officer of inspector rank or above who has reasonable grounds for believing that the detainee:
  (i) may have swallowed a Class A drug; and
  (ii) was in possession of that Class A drug with the intention of supplying it to another or to export; and
(b) the detainee's appropriate consent has been given in writing.

Cannabis resin is a Class B drug so an X-ray or ultrasound scan could not be carried out in these circumstances, making answers A, C and D incorrect.

Evidence and Procedure, para. 2.6.27

87. Answer **C** — The suspect is not allowed to be present when the images are shown to an eye-witness, making answer A incorrect. Answer B is incorrect as although the solicitor is not allowed to communicate with the witness, he/she would be allowed to communicate with the identification officer. A supervised viewing of the recording of the video identification procedure by the suspect and/or their solicitor may be arranged on request, at the discretion of the investigating officer not the identification officer, making answer D incorrect. Answer C is correct as a suspect's solicitor may only be present at the video identification on request and with the prior agreement of the identification officer, if the officer is satisfied that the solicitor's presence will not deter or distract any eye-witness from viewing the images and making an identification.

Evidence and Procedure, para. 2.7.8

88. Answer **C** — PACE84, s. 61A, provides the power for a police officer to take footwear impressions without consent from any person over the age of 10 years who is detained at a police station:

(a) in consequence of being arrested for a recordable offence; or if the detainee has been charged with a recordable offence, or informed they will be reported for such an offence; and

(b) the detainee has not had an impression of their footwear taken in the course of the investigation of the offence unless the previously taken impression is not complete or is not of sufficient quality to allow satisfactory analysis, comparison or matching (whether in the case in question or generally).

Answer C is correct as no consent is required (answers A and B are incorrect in that regard) and the footwear impressions can be taken (answer D is incorrect).

Evidence and Procedure, para. 2.7.5

89. Answer **B** — Section 40 of PACE84 sets out the times when reviews must be conducted. In the case of a person who has been arrested but not charged (WEBSTER), the second review shall not be later than nine hours after the first. The first review was carried out at 14.00hrs that day so the second review shall not be later than nine hours after that (23.00hrs), making answers A, C and D incorrect.

Evidence and Procedure, para. 2.6.18

90. Answer **C** — The right of a detained person to have someone informed of their whereabouts can be delayed if an officer of the rank of inspector or above authorises it, making answers B and D incorrect. The right cannot be delayed beyond 36 hours after the relevant time (para. 4 of Annex B), making answer A incorrect.

Evidence and Procedure, paras 2.6.10, 2.6.23

91. Answer **D** — The question as to whether or not sureties are necessary is at the discretion of the custody officer (or court) which makes answer C incorrect. Answer A is incorrect as s. 8(1) states that this section applies where a person is granted bail in criminal proceedings on condition that they provide *one or more surety or sureties* for the purpose of securing that they surrender to custody. It is not necessary to prove that the surety had any involvement in the accused's non-appearance (*R* v *Warwick Crown Court, ex parte Smalley* [1987] 1 WLR 237), making answer B incorrect. Answer D is the correct answer as s. 8(2) states that in considering the suitability for that purpose of a proposed surety, regard may be had (amongst other things) to:

(a) the surety's financial resources;
(b) his/her character and any previous convictions of his/her; and
(c) his/her proximity (whether in point of kinship, place of residence or otherwise) to the person for whom he/she is to be surety.

Evidence and Procedure, para. 2.2.7.4

92. Answer **D** — The basic period of detention is 24 hours. This can be extended by a superintendent to 36 hours. After this, a warrant of further detention can extend the detention for another 36 hours. Further applications can be made by the police and detention can be extended up to a maximum total of 96 hours.

Evidence and Procedure, para. 2.6.18

93. Answer **D** — Answer B is incorrect as s. 14ZA of the Public Order Act 1986 provides powers to deal with 'one-person' protests. Section 14ZA states:

(1) Subsection (2) applies if the senior police officer, having regard to the time or place at which and the circumstances in which any one-person protest in England and Wales is being carried on or is intended to be carried on, reasonably believes—
  (a) that the noise generated by the person carrying on the protest may result in serious disruption to the activities of an organisation which are carried on in the vicinity of the protest, or
  (b) that—
    (i) the noise generated by the person carrying on the protest may have a relevant impact on persons in the vicinity of the protest, and
    (ii) that impact may be significant.

The provisions of s. 14ZA(1) do not require any reasonable belief in relation to serious public order or damage to property in order to impose them (answer C is incorrect). Answer A is incorrect as the 'senior police officer' means, in relation to a one-person protest being held or to a one-person protest intended to be held in a case where a person is in a place with a view to carrying on such a protest, the most senior in rank of the police officers present at the scene, or in any other case the chief officer of police (s. 14ZA(5)). Answer D is correct as s. 14ZA(2) states that the senior police officer may give directions imposing on the person organising or carrying on the protest such conditions as appear to the officer necessary to prevent such disruption or impact.

General Police Duties, para. 3.8.4.5

94. Answer **B** — The Criminal Justice and Immigration Act 2008, s. 119 states:

(1) A person commits an offence if—
  (a) the person causes, without reasonable excuse and while on NHS premises, a nuisance or disturbance to an NHS staff member who is working there or otherwise there in connection with work,
  (b) the person refuses, without reasonable excuse, to leave the NHS premises when asked to do so by a constable or an NHS staff member, and
  (c) the person is not on the NHS premises for the purpose of obtaining medical advice, treatment or care for himself or herself.

Patients do not commit this offence (answer A is therefore wrong). A person ceases to be on NHS premises for the purpose of obtaining medical advice, treatment or care for him/herself once the person has received the advice, treatment or care. Also, a person is not on NHS premises for the purpose of obtaining medical advice, treatment or care for him/herself if the person has been refused the advice, treatment or care during the last eight hours (s. 119(3)). So KEYSE is not on the premises for the purpose of obtaining medical advice, treatment or care for himself (making answer D incorrect). The behaviour towards a patient would not be caught (making answer D incorrect)—the offence is committed in relation to the behaviour towards RUDD (correct answer B).

General Police Duties, para. 3.5.9

95. Answer **B** — The Police (Conduct) Regulations 2020 define misconduct and the available misconduct sanctions including the Reflective Practice Review, for addressing low-level misconduct as a performance issue. Misconduct is defined as a breach of the Standards of Professional Behaviour that is so serious as to justify disciplinary action. The lowest misconduct sanction now available is a written warning—so that misconduct is a breach of the Standards so serious as to justify a written warning. If the level of misconduct is lower than this, it must be addressed in the Reflective Practice Review process. This makes answer A incorrect (and answer B correct). At a management meeting, the sanctions available are a written warning or a final written warning (answers C and D are incorrect).

General Police Duties, paras 3.17.1, 3.17.6.10

96. Answer **A** — The Road Traffic Act 1988, s. 163 states:

(1) A person driving a mechanically propelled vehicle on a road must stop the vehicle on being required to do so by a constable in uniform or a traffic officer.
(2) A person riding a cycle on a road must stop the cycle on being required to do so by a constable in uniform or a traffic officer.
(3) If a person fails to comply with this section he is guilty of an offence.

The power is therefore available to the officer (s. 163(2)) making answers B, C and D incorrect.

General Police Duties, para. 3.20.2

97. Answer **D** — Section 3 states that it is an offence to engage or take part in chanting of an indecent or racialist nature at a designated football match. For this purpose, 'chanting' means the repeated uttering of any words or sounds (whether alone or in concert with one or more others) and 'of a racialist' nature means consisting of or including matter which is threatening, abusive or insulting to a person by reason of his/her colour, race, nationality (including citizenship) or ethnic or national origins. Answer A is incorrect as s. 1(2) of the 1991 Act provides that references to things done at a 'designated football match' include anything done at the ground within the period beginning two hours before the start of the match or (if earlier) two hours before the time at which it is advertised to start and ending one hour after the end of the match. 'Chanting' can be by one person (answer B is incorrect) but it requires 'repeating' so answer C is incorrect (the offence is committed when KATO repeats the words—correct answer D).

General Police Duties, para. 3.10.3

98. Answer **C** — Code A of the Codes of Practice (para. 4.5) states that a record is required for each person and each vehicle searched. However, if a person is in a vehicle and both are searched, and the object and grounds of the search are the same, only one record needs to be completed (meaning answer B is incorrect). Answer D is incorrect as no such notice is required (it is if you are searching an unattended vehicle—see Code A, para. 4.8). Answer A is incorrect as if a vehicle is searched and a record of the search has been made, then the owner of the vehicle which was searched or the person who was in charge of the vehicle at the time when it was searched is entitled to a copy of the record of search if they ask for one (s. 3(8))—the entitlement to a copy of the search record will run for three months beginning on the date on which the search was made (s. 3(9)), this means answer C is correct.

General Police Duties, para. 3.1.6

99. Answer **B** — Section 51 of the Criminal Justice and Public Order Act 1994 states:

(1) A person commits an offence if—
  (a) he does an act which intimidates, and is intended to intimidate, another person ('the victim'),
  (b) he does the act knowing or believing that the victim is assisting in the investigation of an offence or is a witness or *potential witness* or a juror or potential juror in proceedings for an offence, and
  (c) he does it intending thereby to cause the investigation or the course of justice to be obstructed, perverted or interfered with.

(2) A person commits an offence if—
  (a) he does an act which harms, and is intended to harm, another person or, intending to cause another person to fear harm, he threatens to do an act which would harm that other person,
  (b) he does or threatens to do the act knowing or believing that the person harmed or threatened to be harmed ('the victim'), or some other person, *has assisted* in an investigation into an offence or *has given evidence or particular evidence* in proceedings for an offence, or *has acted* as a juror or concurred in a particular verdict in proceedings for an offence, and
  (c) he does or threatens to do it because of that knowledge or belief.

(3) For the purposes of subsections (1) and (2) it is immaterial that the act is or would be done, or that the threat is made—
  (a) otherwise than in the presence of the victim, or
  (b) to a person other than the victim.

(4) The harm that may be done or threatened may be financial as well as physical (whether to the person or a person's property) and similarly as respects an intimidatory act which consists of threats.

The offence can be committed against a 'potential witness', making answer A incorrect. The victim of the offence does not actually have to be intimidated, so even if the victim is not in fear, the offence can be made out, making answer C incorrect. In this question, the offence is committed when WARD makes the threat to AGNEW regarding wages and also when he threatens AGNEW with violence. Answer D is incorrect as AGNEW has not actually assisted in an investigation etc.

General Police Duties, para. 3.14.5.1

100. Answer **C** — PACE84, s. 18 states:

(1) Subject to the following provisions of this section, a constable may enter and search any premises occupied or controlled by a person who is under arrest for an indictable offence, if he has reasonable grounds for suspecting that there is on the premises evidence, other than items subject to legal privilege, that relates—
  (a) to that offence; or
  (b) to some other indictable offence which is connected with or similar to that offence.

(2) A constable may seize and retain anything for which he may search under subsection (1) above.

(3) The power to search conferred by subsection (1) above is only a power to search to the extent that is reasonably required for the purpose of discovering such evidence.

(4) Subject to subsection (5) below, the powers conferred by this section may not be exercised unless an officer of the rank of inspector or above has authorised them in writing.

(5) A constable may conduct a search under subsection (1)—

(a) before the person is taken to a police station or released on bail under section 30A; and

(b) without obtaining an authorisation under subsection (4), if the condition in subsection (5A) is satisfied.

(5A) The condition is that the presence of the person at a place (other than a police station) is necessary for the effective investigation of the offence.

(6) If a constable conducts a search by virtue of subsection (5) above, he shall inform an officer of the rank of inspector or above that he has made the search as soon as practicable after he has made it.

The person does not need to be in 'police detention' (incorrect answer B) nor (if ss. 5 and 5A are satisfied) does an officer of the rank of inspector or above need to authorise the search—making answers A and D incorrect. The circumstances satisfy ss. 5 and 5A so the search can take place (correct answer C).

General Police Duties, para. 3.2.7

101. Answer **D** — The offence of misconduct in a public office applies to any person holding a public office and AUSTIN would be included in that category. In *R* v *Bowden* [1996] 1 WLR 98, a man employed by a local council as a maintenance manager dishonestly caused his employees to carry out works on his girlfriend's premises and committed the offence, making answers A and B incorrect. To prove the offence, a number of factors must be established including evidence of wilful neglect and/or wilful misconduct. Simple inadvertence or accidental action/omission without more will not be enough (*Attorney-General's Reference (No. 3 of 2003)* [2004] EWCA Crim 868) meaning that PC KROHN will not have committed the offence and making answer C incorrect.

General Police Duties, para. 3.18.17.1

102. Answer **C** — The offence under s. 3A is committed if a person causes the death of another person by driving a mechanically propelled vehicle on a road or other public place without due care and attention, or without reasonable consideration for other persons using the road or place, and:

(a) he is, at the time when he is driving, unfit to drive through drink or drugs, or

(b) he has consumed so much alcohol that the proportion of it in his breath, blood or urine at that time exceeds the prescribed limit, or

(ba) he has in his body a specified controlled drug and the proportion of it in his blood or urine at that time exceeds the specified limit for that drug, or

(c) he is, within 18 hours after that time, required to provide a specimen in pursuance of section 7 of this Act, but without reasonable excuse fails to provide it, or

(d) he is required by a constable to give his permission for a laboratory test of a specimen of blood taken from him under section 7A of this Act, but without reasonable excuse fails to do so, he is guilty of an offence.

McNAMARA would be caught by s. 3A(c). Answer A is incorrect as the requirement under s. 3A(1)(c) is for the provision of a specimen for analysis under s. 7 of the Road Traffic Act

1988 and not a screening test under s. 6. The fact that McNAMARA might be under the limit etc. is irrelevant (answer B) as the offence is committed by failing, without reasonable excuse, to provide a specimen under s. 7—McNAMARA has failed to provide. Answer D is incorrect as the death of 'another' would include a foetus which was later born alive but which subsequently died.

General Police Duties, paras 3.21.2.1, 3.21.5, 3.21.6.1

103. Answer **A** — Section 1(4) of PACE84 states that if a person is in a garden or yard occupied with and used for the purposes of a dwelling or on other land so occupied and used, a constable *may not* search him/her in the exercise of the power conferred by this section *unless* the constable has reasonable grounds for believing:

(a) that he/she does not reside in the dwelling; and
(b) that he/she is not in the place in question with the express or implied permission of a person who resides in the dwelling.

So the power is available if the officer reasonably believes s. 1(4)(a) or (b) above. This means that answer B is incorrect. Answers C and D are incorrect as the power under s. 1 of PACE84 is *not available in a dwelling in any circumstances* (regardless of the officer's mindset etc.). If the officers reasonably believe s. 1(4)(a) and (b), they can search DOVE but, as you can never use s. 1 in a dwelling, it means that answer A is correct.

General Police Duties, para. 3.1.4

104. Answer **C** — The Criminal Justice and Public Order Act 1994, s. 61 states:

(1) If the senior police officer present at the scene reasonably believes that two or more persons are trespassing on land and are present there with the common purpose of residing there for any period, that reasonable steps have been taken by or on behalf of the occupier to ask them to leave and—
   (a) that any of those persons
      (i) in the case of persons trespassing on land in England and Wales, has caused damage, disruption or distress (see subsection 10);
      (ii) in the case of persons trespassing on the land in Scotland,
   has caused to damage to the land or to property on the land or used threatening, abusive or insulting words or behaviour towards the occupier, a member of his family or an employee or agent of his, or
   (b) in either case those persons have between them six or more vehicles on the land, he may direct those persons, or any of them, to leave the land and to remove any vehicles or other property they have with them on the land.

The direction can be given if the circumstances at s. 61(1)(a) or (b) apply, meaning that answer B is incorrect. The direction can be given to two or more persons, making answer D incorrect. It can be given if any of those persons has caused damage, disruption or distress and using threatening, abusive or insulting words or behaviour would amount to such 'distress', so answer A is incorrect.

General Police Duties, para. 3.5.5

105. Answer **B** — The Domestic Abuse Act 2021 provides the statutory definition of domestic abuse and s. 1 states:

(1) This section defines 'domestic abuse' for the purposes of this Act.
(2) Behaviour of a person ('A') towards another person ('B') is 'domestic abuse' if—
 (a) A and B are each aged 16 or over and are personally connected to each other, and
 (b) the behaviour is abusive.
(3) Behaviour is 'abusive' if it consists of any of the following—
 (a) physical or sexual abuse;
 (b) violent or threatening behaviour;
 (c) controlling or coercive behaviour;
 (d) economic abuse (see subsection (4));
 (e) psychological, emotional or other abuse;
 and it does not matter whether the behaviour consists of a single incident or a course of conduct.

The above makes answers C and D incorrect.

In relation to s. 1(2)(a) above, the Domestic Abuse Act 2021, s. 2 states:

(1) For the purposes of this Act, two people are 'personally connected' to each other if any of the following applies—
 (a) they are, or have been, married to each other;
 (b) they are, or have been, civil partners of each other;
 (c) they have agreed to marry one another (whether or not the agreement has been terminated);
 (d) they have entered into a civil partnership agreement (whether or not the agreement has been terminated);
 (e) they are, or have been, in an intimate personal relationship with each other;
 (f) they each have, or there has been a time when they each have had, a parental relationship in relation to the same child (see subsection (2));
 (g) they are relatives.
(2) For the purposes of subsection (1)(f) a person has a parental relationship in relation to a child if—
 (a) the person is a parent of the child, or
 (b) the person has parental responsibility for the child.

This means that answer A is incorrect and that answer B (they are brother and sister and are relatives) is correct (s. 2(g)).

General Police Duties, para. 3.11.2

106. Answer **B** — Preliminary tests can be required and administered in a variety of circumstances.

Regardless of those circumstances, the officer *making the requirement* for the preliminary test to take place *does not have to be in uniform*—an officer in plain clothes can make the requirement which eliminates answers A and C. The officer administering a preliminary test (breath test, drug test or impairment test) must be in uniform (s. 6(7) of the Act); however, this uniform requirement only applies to preliminary tests administered under s. 6(2) to (4) of the Act—it does not apply in cases of preliminary tests following an accident (s. 6(5) of the Act). Section 6 of the Road Traffic Act 1988 states:

(5) This subsection applies if—
   (a) an accident occurs owing to the presence of a motor vehicle on a road or other public place, and
   (b) a constable reasonably believes that the person was driving, attempting to drive or in charge of the vehicle at the time of the accident.

There is no need for the police officer making the requirement to believe or even suspect that the person has been drinking, or that he/she has committed any offence; reasonable belief in his/her involvement (as a person driving, attempting to drive or being in charge of a vehicle) in the accident is enough. There is also no need for the officer administering the test to be in uniform, making answer D incorrect.

General Police Duties, paras 3.22.4 to 3.22.4.3

107. Answer **C** — Section 24 of PACE84 provides seven scenarios where a constable has a power of arrest—these can be divided into three time frames and if the mind-set of the arresting officer is mentioned that will only ever be one of 'suspicion' (not belief—ruling out answers A and D):

Offence Time Frame	**Police Powers of Arrest under s. 24 PACE84**
PAST	1. If a constable has reasonable grounds for suspecting that an offence *has been committed*, he/she may arrest without a warrant anyone whom he/she has reasonable grounds to suspect of being guilty of it (s. 24(2)). 2. If an offence *has been committed*, a constable may arrest anyone without a warrant who is guilty of the offence (s. 24(3)(a)). 3. If an offence *has been committed*, a constable may arrest anyone without warrant whom he/she has reasonable grounds for suspecting to be guilty of it (s. 24(3)(b)).
PRESENT	4. A constable may arrest without warrant anyone *who is in the act of committing* an offence (s. 24(1)(b)). 5. A constable may arrest without warrant anyone whom he/she has reasonable grounds for suspecting *to be committing* an offence (s. 24(1)(d)).
FUTURE	6. A constable may arrest without warrant anyone who is *about to commit* an offence (s. 24(1)(a)). 7. A constable may arrest without warrant anyone whom he/she has reasonable grounds for suspecting to be *about to commit* an offence (s. 24(1(c)).

The situations at 6 and 7 relate to 'anticipated' offences (making answer B incorrect). The situation described in the circumstances of the MCQ would fall into the seventh category (correct answer C).

General Police Duties, para. 3.3.4

108. Answer **A** — Section 6(5) of the Road Traffic Act 1988 states that if an accident occurs owing to the presence of a motor vehicle on a road or other public place and a constable reasonably believes that the person was driving, attempting to drive or in charge of the vehicle at the time of the accident, then the officer can require the person to cooperate with one or more of the

preliminary tests. There is no need, under s. 6(5), for the officer making the requirement to be in uniform, meaning that answer B is incorrect. The word 'accident' is interpreted widely and an incident where the only person injured was the driver of the motor vehicle or the only vehicle damaged was that motor vehicle would still be considered an 'accident', making answer C incorrect. If PC ASKEW made the requirement and CORK took and failed the preliminary breath test, he could not be arrested under s. 6D of the Road Traffic Act 1988. Section 6D provides a power of arrest but s. 6D(3) specifically forbids the arrest of a person whilst they are at a hospital as a patient, making answer D incorrect. PC ASKEW would be allowed to make the requirement for the provision of the preliminary breath test if the medical practitioner in immediate charge of CORK's case has been notified of the proposal to make the requirement and does not object to the requirement being made (s. 9(1) of the Road Traffic Act 1988), making A the correct answer.

General Police Duties, paras 3.22.4.3, 3.22.4.5, 3.22.6

109. Answer **D** — PACE84, s. 32 states:

(1) A constable may search an arrested person, in any case where the person to be searched *has been arrested at a place other than a police station*, if the constable has reasonable grounds for believing that the arrested person may present a danger to himself or others.
(2) Subject to subsections (3) to (5) below, a constable shall also have power in any such case—
  (a) to search the arrested person for anything—
    (i) which he might use to assist him to escape from lawful custody; or
    (ii) which might be evidence relating to an offence; and
  (b) if the offence for which he has been arrested is an indictable offence, to enter and search any premises in which he was when arrested or immediately before he was arrested for evidence relating to the offence.

As FOGARTY was arrested at a police station, the power under s. 32 is not available to PC MARRI (correct answer D).

General Police Duties, para. 3.2.7

110. Answer **C** — The Protection from Harassment Act 1997, s. 1 states:

(1) A person must not pursue a course of conduct—
  (a) which amounts to harassment of another, and
  (b) which he knows or ought to know amounts to harassment of the other.
(1A) A person must not pursue a course of conduct—
  (a) which involves harassment of two or more persons, and
  (b) which he knows or ought to know involves harassment of those persons, and
  (c) by which he intends to persuade any person (whether or not one of those mentioned above)—
    (i) not to do something that he is entitled or required to do, or
    (ii) to do something that he is not under any obligation to do.

Answer B is incorrect as 'harassment' does not require any threats of violence. 'Person' here does not include companies or corporate bodies and therefore they cannot be the 'direct' *victim* of harassment or apply for injunctions as a 'victim' of harassment under this part of the legislation (it is a requirement that there must be evidence of harassment of an individual ('natural') person(s) and not just a corporate body (s. 7(5)). This rules out WBI Construction Ltd as a 'person' who can be harassed and means the only form of harassment to be considered would be under s. 1. Answer A is incorrect as 'harassment' includes alarming the person or causing him/her distress (s. 7(2) of the 1997 Act). Although the words used in s. 7 are 'alarm *and* distress', the Divisional Court has held that they should be taken disjunctively and not conjunctively, that is, the court need only be satisfied that the behaviour involved one or the other; alarm *or* distress (*DPP* v *Ramsdale* [2001] EWHC Admin 106). Answer D is incorrect as whilst 'conduct' includes speech (see s. 7(4) of the Act), it is not a requirement that the harassment takes that form (there are numerous case law examples in the *General Police Duties Manual* where sending letters amounts to harassment). A 'course of conduct' by a person is defined under s. 7 of the Act which states:

(3) A 'course of conduct' must involve—
  (a) in the case of conduct in relation to a single person (see section 1(1)), conduct on at least two occasions in relation to that person, or
  (b) in the case of conduct in relation to two or more persons (see section 1(1A)), conduct on at least one occasion in relation to each of those persons.

As this is an incident involving a single person, the offence would not be committed (it has only happened on one occasion—correct answer C).

General Police Duties, paras 3.12.4 to 3.12.4.3

111. Answer **C** — The 'specified period' of an improvement notice is a period specified by the manager conducting the meeting (having considered any representations made by or on behalf of the police officer) within which the police officer must improve his/her performance or attendance. It is expected that the specified period for improvement would not normally exceed *three months* (correct answer C). This makes answer A incorrect. Answer B is incorrect as on the application of the police officer or otherwise (e.g. on the application of his/her line manager), the appropriate authority may extend the specified period, if it considers it appropriate to do so. In setting an extension to the specified period, consideration should be given to any known periods of extended absence from the police officer's normal role, e.g. if the police officer is going to be on long periods of pre-planned holiday leave, study leave or is due to undergo an operation. The extension should not lead to the improvement period exceeding *12 months* (making answer D incorrect) unless the appropriate authority is satisfied that there are exceptional circumstances making this appropriate.

General Police Duties, para. 3.18.9.2

112. Answer **C** — The Confiscation of Alcohol (Young Persons) Act 1997, s. 1 states:

(1) Where a constable reasonably suspects that a person in a relevant place is in possession of alcohol, and that either—
  (a) he is under the age of 18; or
  (b) he intends that any of the alcohol should be consumed by a person under the age of 18 in that or any other relevant place; or
  (c) a person under the age of 18 who is, or has recently been, with him has recently consumed alcohol in that or any other relevant place,

  the constable may require him to surrender anything in his possession which is, or which the constable reasonably believes to be, alcohol or a container for alcohol.

So under s. 1(1), PC BUNN can require the surrender of the opened and unopened cans of cider, making answer B incorrect. Under s. 1(2), the officer may dispose of anything surrendered to him/her in answer to the making of the requirement, making answer D incorrect. Under s. 1(1AB), a constable who imposes a requirement on a person under subs. (1) may, if the constable reasonably suspects that the person is under the age of 16, remove the person to the person's place of residence or a place of safety, making answer A incorrect. Although a 'place of safety' is not defined, this may be a relative or friend or, where necessary, *a police station* or social services accommodation (correct answer C).

General Police Duties, para. 3.6.6.3

113. Answer **D** — Violence does not need to be used, threatened or feared in order for an offence of stalking (under s. 2A of the Protection from Harassment Act 1997) to be committed, making answers A and C incorrect. The offence does require a 'course of conduct in breach of section 1(1)' which will, with regards to conduct in relation to a single person, be conduct on at least two occasions—this rules out answer B. The offence is committed when the second activity takes place (stalking behaviour includes following a person and watching or spying on a person).

General Police Duties, paras 3.12.4.2, 3.12.6.1

114. Answer **A** — The Criminal Justice and Public Order Act 1994, s. 69 states:

(1) If the senior police officer present at the scene reasonably believes—
(a) that a person is committing, has committed or intends to commit the offence of aggravated trespass on land; or
(b) that two or more persons are trespassing on land and are present there with the common purpose of intimidating persons so as to deter them from engaging in a lawful activity or of obstructing or disrupting a lawful activity, he may direct that person or (as the case may be) those persons (or any of them) to leave the land.

There is no requirement for the officer giving the direction to be in uniform (answer C is incorrect)—the 'senior officer present at the scene' (correct answer A) gives the direction not a superintendent or an inspector (incorrect answers B and D).

General Police Duties, para. 3.5.2.1

115. Answer **A** — Answer A is correct as the officer directing that the powers conferred by s. 16 shall be exercisable will be an officer of the rank of superintendent or above. Answer B is incorrect as the powers apply where the officer has 'reasonable cause to believe' not suspect. Answer C is incorrect as there is no requirement for the constable exercising the power to be in uniform. Answer D is incorrect as the power is available in a public place only.

General Police Duties, para. 3.7.12

116. Answer **B** — The Public Order Act 1986, s. 4 states:

(1) A person is guilty of an offence if he—
(a) uses towards another person threatening, abusive or insulting words or behaviour, or
(b) distributes or displays to another person any writing, sign or other visible representation which is threatening, abusive or insulting, with intent to cause that person to believe that immediate unlawful violence will be used against him or

another by any person, or to provoke the immediate use of unlawful violence by that person or another, or whereby that person is likely to believe that such violence will be used or it is likely that such violence will be provoked.

The offence can place in public or in private (answer D is incorrect) and the requirement for 'immediacy' eliminates answer A. Answer C is incorrect as s. 4(2) states that an offence under this section may be committed in a public or a private place, except that no offence is committed where the words or behaviour are used, or the writing, sign or other visible representation is distributed or displayed, by a person inside a dwelling and the other person is also inside that or another dwelling (correct answer B).

General Police Duties, para. 3.9.6

117. Answer **B** — Section 1(5) of the Public Order Act 1986 states that the offence of riot can be committed in public or private, making answer A incorrect. The offence under s. 1(1) states that where 12 or more persons who are present together use or threaten unlawful violence for a common purpose and the conduct of them (taken together) is such as would cause a person of reasonable firmness present at the scene to fear for their personal safety, each of the persons *using unlawful violence* for the common purpose is guilty of riot. An important point to note is that it is only the persons *using* violence who can be guilty of the offence of riot. You do require 12 or more persons present together for riot but they do not all need to use violence, making answer C incorrect. As it is those who use violence who commit the offence, this makes answer D incorrect and answer B correct.

General Police Duties, para. 3.9.3

118. Answer **A** — Section 6(5) of the Road Traffic Act 1988 states that if an accident occurs owing to the presence of a motor vehicle on a road or other public place and a constable reasonably believes that the person was driving, attempting to drive or in charge of the vehicle at the time of the accident, they may require a preliminary test to take place. You must show that an accident has taken place, not simply believe that to be the case. Answer B is incorrect as, apart from the fact that the requirement cannot be made, the preliminary test may take place at or near the place where the requirement to cooperate with the test is imposed *or*, if the constable who imposes the requirement thinks it expedient to do so, at a police station specified by him/her. Answer C is incorrect as if an accident has taken place there is no need for the officer making the requirement to believe or even suspect that the person has been drinking. Answer D is incorrect as there is no need for the officer to believe or suspect that any offence has taken place.

General Police Duties, para. 3.22.4.3

119. Answer **D** — Answer A is incorrect as, while suspended, a police officer ceases to hold the office of constable and, in the case of a member of a police force, ceases to be a member of a police force, save for the purposes of the misconduct proceedings: PCR, reg. 11(1), (2). Answer B is incorrect as the use of suspension must be reviewed at least every four weeks, and sooner where facts have become known which suggest that suspension is no longer appropriate: PCR, reg. 11(8). Answer C is incorrect as suspension must be authorised by a senior officer (which is an officer holding a rank above that of chief superintendent) (PCR,

reg. 2(4)(a)). The Standards of Professional Behaviour continue to apply to police officers who are suspended from duty: PCR, reg. 11(2) (correct answer D).

General Police Duties, para. 3.17.5.1

120. Answer **C** — Answer A is incorrect as a breach of the peace can take place in private as well as in public. Answer B is incorrect as a breach of the peace occurs when an act is done, or threatened to be done:

- which harms a person or, in his/her presence, his/her property; or
- which is likely to cause such harm; or
- which puts someone in fear of such harm.

A person arrested for a breach of the peace is not in police detention and the provisions in relation to bail do not apply, making answer D incorrect. After being arrested, a person may be detained and placed before the next available court, or detained until there is no further likelihood of a reoccurrence of the breach of the peace.

General Police Duties, paras 3.9.2 to 3.9.2.4

121. Answer **D** — Powers to enter under s. 17 are available to officers for many reasons. Pursuing a person who is unlawfully at large and whom the officer is pursuing is one of those reasons (s. 17(1)(d)) as is the power to enter, search and arrest for an indictable offence (s. 17(1)(b))—but these are not the only reasons an officer may enter under s. 17, meaning that answers B and C are incorrect. PACE84, s. 17(1)(c)(iii) states that a constable may enter and search any premises for the purpose of arresting a person for an offence under s. 4 of the Public Order Act 1986 (fear or provocation of violence). The officer does not have to be in uniform to exercise the power under s. 17(1)(c)(iii), making answer A incorrect. Force may be used if necessary, meaning that answer D is correct.

General Police Duties, para. 3.2.7

122. Answer **B** — Section 4(1A) of the Criminal Law Act 1967 states that a 'relevant offence' means:

(a) an offence for which the sentence is fixed by law,
(b) an offence for which a person of 18 years or over (not previously convicted) may be sentenced to imprisonment for a term of five years (or might be so sentenced but for the restrictions imposed by section 33 of the Magistrates' Courts Act 1980).

Theft is an offence punishable by a term of seven years' imprisonment on conviction making it a 'relevant offence' and making answer D incorrect. This offence must involve some positive act by the defendant; saying or doing nothing will not suffice, making answer A incorrect. For the offence to exist, the defendant must know or believe the assisted person to be guilty of the offence or some relevant offence. Mere suspicion, however strong, that the 'assisted' person had committed a relevant offence will not be enough which means that answer B is correct and that answer C is incorrect.

General Police Duties, para. 3.14.7

123. Answer **C** — Answer D is incorrect as a criminal behaviour order (CBO) means an order for the purpose of preventing an offender from engaging in behaviour that is likely to cause

harassment, alarm or distress to any person (not violent behaviour). The CBO is an order 'on conviction' not as an alternative to it (answer A is incorrect). The order can be made by the Crown Court, magistrates' court or youth court (STEDDING can be subject to a CBO so answer B is incorrect). For an offender who has reached the age of 18, the order period must be a fixed period of not less than two years or an indefinite period (s. 334(5)—correct answer C).

General Police Duties, paras 3.7.4 to 3.7.4.2

124. Answer **A** — Special safeguards apply in relation to the authorisation of juveniles and vulnerable individuals as 'CHIS'. Juveniles are those under 18 years of age. On no occasion should the use or conduct of a CHIS under 16 years of age be authorised to give information against their parents or any person who has parental responsibility for them (but this would not stop OTTER providing information about his uncle, making answer D incorrect). Answer B is incorrect as although a person under 16 cannot be used as a CHIS to provide information about their parents or a person with parental responsibility for them, this does not stop those under 16 being a CHIS (albeit that authorisations should not be granted unless the special provisions contained within the Regulation of Investigatory Powers (Juveniles) (Amendment) Order 2018 (SI 2018/715) are satisfied).

A CHIS authorisation for a juvenile/vulnerable CHIS lasts four months beginning on the day authorisation is granted (making answer C incorrect).

General Police Duties, para. 3.13.5.4

125. Answer **A** — The reasons for seizure are contained in s. 19(2) and (3)—they are both driven by an officer's reasonable belief (not suspicion, answer B is incorrect). Section 19(2) is that it has been obtained in consequence of the commission of an offence and the property should be seized in order to prevent it from being concealed, lost, damaged, altered or destroyed and s. 19(3) is that it is evidence in relation to an offence and it should be seized in order to prevent it from being concealed, lost, altered or destroyed (so answer C is incorrect). Paragraph 7.6 of Code B reflects the provisions of s. 20 of PACE84 (extension of powers of seizure to computerised information). This states that where a power of seizure exists under any enactment (such as s. 19 of PACE84), there will also be a power to require any information stored in any electronic form and accessible from the premises to be produced in a form in which it can be taken away and in which it is visible and legible (correct answer A) or from which it can readily be produced in a visible and legible form (s. 20(1)), making answer D incorrect.

General Police Duties, para. 3.2.10

126. Answer **B** — There are a variety of reasons allowing a court to make a parenting order (e.g. a child safety order has been made in respect of the child), not just the fact that the child or young person in question has been convicted of an offence, making answer A incorrect (s. 8(1) of the Crime and Disorder Act 1998). A court does not have to bind GIBSON over, although if it does not, it will have to state in open court why that is the case (s. 376(4)(b) of the Sentencing Act 2020), making answer D incorrect. The recognisance can be imposed on the parent or guardian; the period of a recognisance under this section may not be more three years and must end before the offender reaches the age of 18 (s. 376(7)), making

answer C incorrect. A parenting order lasts for a period not exceeding 12 months (correct answer B) (s. 8(4) of the Crime and Disorder Act 1998).

General Police Duties, paras 3.7.10.1 to 3.7.10.2

127. Answer **A** — Under s. 165A of the Road Traffic Act 1988, a police officer has the power to seize a vehicle if he/she has reasonable grounds for believing that the driver does not have a suitable licence or that the vehicle is not adequately insured. To seize a vehicle, a police officer must be in uniform and have requested to see the relevant documents. He/she must also warn the driver that the vehicle will be seized unless the documents are produced immediately (however, if it is impractical to warn the driver then a warning is not required (s. 165A(6))). If the driver has failed to stop or has driven off, the vehicle may be seized at any time in the 24-hour period following the incident (making answers B and D incorrect as the vehicle cannot be seized). A police officer has the legal power to enter premises to seize a vehicle, including from a driveway or garage associated with a private dwelling-house (answer C is incorrect). The officer must have reasonable grounds for believing the vehicle to be present, and reasonable force may be used if necessary.

General Police Duties, para. 3.20.6

128. Answer **A** — Section 1A of the Sporting Events (Control of Alcohol etc.) Act 1985 states:

(1) This section applies to a motor vehicle which—
  (a) is not a public service vehicle but is adapted to carry more than 8 passengers, and
  (b) is being used for the principal purpose of carrying two or more passengers for the whole or part of a journey to or from a designated sporting event.
(2) A person who knowingly causes or permits alcohol to be carried on a motor vehicle to which this section applies is guilty of an offence—
  (a) if he is its driver, or
  (b) if he is not its driver but is its keeper, the servant or agent of its keeper, a person to whom it is made available (by hire, loan or otherwise) by its keeper or the keeper's servant or agent, or the servant or agent of a person to whom it is so made available.
(3) A person who has alcohol in his possession while on a motor vehicle to which this section applies is guilty of an offence.
(4) A person who is drunk on a motor vehicle to which this section applies is guilty of an offence.

If the vehicle in question was adapted to carry more than eight passengers, then all three of the named individuals would commit the offence—but it is only adapted to carry six passengers and the driver so the s. 1A offence would not apply to the vehicle and occupants, meaning that answers B, C and D are incorrect.

General Police Duties, para. 3.10.5.2

129. Answer **D** — The power of search under s. 136C does not authorise a constable to require a person to remove any of their clothing other than an outer coat, jacket or gloves (answer B is incorrect) but does authorise a search of a person's mouth (s. 136C(3)—correct answer D). It is a power available to a constable (answer A is incorrect). Where a person is detained under a warrant issued under s. 135(1) or (2) *or* a power under s. 136(2) or (4), a constable may search the person, at any time while the person is so detained, if the constable has

reasonable grounds for believing that the person may present a danger to themself or to others and is concealing on their person an item that could be used to cause physical injury to themself or to others (answer C is incorrect).

General Police Duties, para. 3.4.2

130. Answer **B** — Answer D is incorrect as s. 28(3) of PACE84 states that no arrest is lawful unless the person arrested is informed of the ground for the arrest at the time of, or as soon as practicable after, the arrest. Further, s. 28(4) states that subs. (3) applies regardless of whether the ground for the arrest is obvious. Answer C is incorrect as in relation to the arrest itself, in *R* v *Fiak* [2005] EWCA Crim 2381 it was held that an arrest had not been rendered unlawful by the police officer's failure to use the word 'arrest'—this requirement might be met by using a colloquialism, provided that the person is familiar with it and understands its meaning (e.g. 'you're locked up' or 'you're nicked' (*Christie* v *Leachinsky* [1947] AC 573)). Code G, para. 2.9 (e)(i) provides examples of when it may be necessary to arrest a person to allow the prompt and effective investigation of the offence which includes the fact that arrest enables a 'special warning' to be given (answer A is incorrect). Suspects must be informed of the reason or reasons why the arrest is considered necessary (correct answer B).

General Police Duties, paras 3.3.4 to 3.3.5

131. Answer **C** — A misconduct meeting shall take place not later than 20 working days beginning with the first working day after the date on which the documents and material for the meeting were supplied to the police officer under reg. 30 of the Police (Conduct) Regulations 2020. The person conducting or chairing the misconduct proceedings may extend the time limit where they consider that this would be in the interests of justice.

General Police Duties, para. 3.17.6.1

132. Answer **C** — Answer A is incorrect as a road check under s. 4 of PACE84 can be authorised for a number of reasons. Section 4(1) states:

(1) This section shall have effect in relation to the conduct of road checks by police officers for the purpose of ascertaining whether a vehicle is carrying—
(a) a person who has committed an offence other than a road traffic offence or a vehicle excise offence;
(b) a person who is a witness to such an offence;
(c) a person intending to commit such an offence; or
(d) a person who is unlawfully at large.

It is correct that a road check should be authorised in writing and if authorised will last for a period of seven days; however, answers B and D are incorrect as a road check will be authorised by an officer of superintendent rank or above.

General Police Duties, para. 3.20.3

133. Answer **B** — Section 30 of PACE84 provides for the procedure to be adopted after a person has been arrested. Section 30 states:

(1) Subsection (1A) applies where a person is, at any place other than a police station—
(a) arrested by a constable for an offence, or

(b) taken into custody by a constable after being arrested for an offence by a person other than a constable.

(1A) The person must be taken by a constable to a police station as soon as practicable after the arrest.

So PACE84 requires that such an arrested person be taken to a *police station*. Section 30(2) states that subject to subss. (3) and (5) of s. 30, the police station to which an arrested person is taken under subs. (1A) above shall be a *designated police station*. However, as there are exceptions to this requirement contained in s. 30(3) and (5), answer A must be incorrect.

Section 30(5) states that any constable may take an arrested person to any police station if:

(a) either of the following conditions is satisfied—
  (i) the constable has arrested him without the assistance of any other constable and no other constable is available to assist him;
  (ii) the constable has taken him into custody from a person other than a constable without the assistance of any other constable and no other constable is available to assist him; and

(b) it appears to the constable that he will be unable to take the arrested person to a designated police station without the arrested person injuring himself, the constable or some other person.

The behaviour of PC CURTIS would be covered by s. 30(5)(a)(i) and (b) so her behaviour is lawful, making answer C incorrect.

Section 30(6) states that if the first police station to which an arrested person is taken after their arrest is not a designated police station, he/she shall be taken to a designated police station not more than six hours after their arrival at the first police station unless he/she is released previously (correct answer B). There is no requirement to contact an inspector and transport the arrested person as soon as practicable as mentioned in the incorrect answer D.

General Police Duties, para. 3.3.11

134. Answer **C** — The Road Traffic Act 1988, s. 10 states:

(1) Subject to subsections (2) and (3) below, a person required under section 7 or 7A to provide a specimen of breath, blood or urine may afterwards be detained at a police station (or, if the specimen was provided otherwise than at a police station, arrested and taken to and detained at a police station) if a constable has reasonable grounds for believing that, were that person then driving or attempting to drive a mechanically propelled vehicle on a road, he would commit an offence under section 4, 5 or 5A of this Act.

The trigger for the power under s. 10 is that a person has been required to provide a specimen of breath, blood or urine under s. 7 or 7A of the Act—not that the offence was drug-related under s. 5A (meaning that answer D is incorrect). A consultation with a medical professional is required if the person's ability to drive properly is or might be impaired through drink or drugs—that is not the case here, making answer B incorrect. The power under s. 10 can be used if a constable believes (not suspects) that were that person then driving or attempting to drive (not just driving) a mechanically propelled vehicle on a road, he/she would commit an offence under s. 4, 5 or 5A (not just s. 5 or 5A)—the incorrect elements of answer A are in the brackets—answer C is therefore correct.

General Police Duties, para. 3.22.7

135. Answer **A** — Answer A is correct as the Anti-social Behaviour, Crime and Policing Act 2014, s. 76 states:

(1) A police officer of at least the rank of inspector [answer C is incorrect], or the local authority, may issue a closure notice if satisfied on reasonable grounds—
  (a) that the use of particular premises has resulted, or (if the notice is not issued) is likely soon to result, in nuisance to members of the public, or
  (b) that there has been, or (if the notice is not issued) is likely soon to be, disorder near those premises associated with the use of those premises, and that the notice is necessary to prevent the nuisance or disorder from continuing, recurring or occurring [answer D is incorrect].

The maximum period that may be specified in a closure notice is 24 hours (s. 77(1)). However, this may be extended to a maximum of 48 hours by an officer of at least the rank of superintendent (s. 77(2)—answer B is incorrect).

General Police Duties, para. 3.7.9.1

136. Answer **D** — Code A of the Codes of Practice applies to all powers of stop and search requiring 'reasonable grounds to suspect' as a basis for the search and therefore applies to a search carried out under s. 1 of PACE84. Code A states that the searching officer can, in public view:

- place his/her hands inside the pockets of outer clothing (so there is nothing wrong with PC CULPAN doing this to FRASER, making answer A incorrect);
- feel round the inside of collars, socks and shoes (para. 3.5);
- search a person's hair, if this does not require the removal of headgear (para. 3.5);
- require the person to remove his/her outer coat, jacket and gloves.

The person *cannot* be required to remove any further clothing in public, but can be asked to remove more clothing voluntarily. If a more thorough search is required, this can be conducted but this must be out of public view, for example in a police van or at a nearby police station, making answer B incorrect. If the search involves removing anything beyond an outer coat, jacket, gloves, headgear or footwear, the searching officer and any other officers present must be of *the same sex* as the person being searched unless the person specifically requests otherwise. This is not the case inside the police van so the search in these circumstances was correct (making answer C incorrect).

General Police Duties, para. 3.1.5

137. Answer **B** — PACE84 makes provision for the so-called citizen's arrest powers. Far narrower than the police powers, these powers of arrest are set out in s. 24A, which states:

(1) A person other than a constable may arrest without a warrant—
  (a) anyone who is in the act of committing an indictable offence;
  (b) anyone whom he has reasonable grounds for suspecting to be committing an indictable offence.

(2) Where an indictable offence has been committed, a person other than a constable may arrest without a warrant—
   (a) anyone who is guilty of the offence;
   (b) anyone whom he has reasonable grounds for suspecting to be guilty of it.
(3) But the power of summary arrest conferred by subsection (1) or (2) is exercisable only if—
   (a) the person making the arrest has reasonable grounds for believing that for any of the reasons mentioned in subsection (4) it is necessary to arrest the person in question; and
   (b) it appears to the person making the arrest that it is not reasonably practicable for a constable to make it instead.
(4) The reasons are to prevent the person in question:
   (a) causing physical injury to himself or any other person;
   (b) suffering physical injury;
   (c) causing loss of or damage to property; or
   (d) making off before a constable can assume responsibility for him.
(5) This section does not apply in relation to an offence under Part 3 or 3A of the Public Order Act 1986.

Unlike the powers of arrest available to police officers (which apply to any and every offence), the citizen's power of arrest only applies where the relevant offence is indictable. This power is available to police staff and others such as Police Community Support Officers (making answer A incorrect). An offence that is triable either way is an 'indictable offence'—this would only exclude offences that are triable summarily only, making answer C incorrect. LORIMER behaved correctly (answer B) as the grounds under s. 24A(1)(b) applied and were accompanied by the element at s. 24A(3) and (4)(b), making answer D incorrect.

General Police Duties, para. 3.3.8

138. Answer **A** — The offence of violent disorder has been committed by all three men in this scenario. The fact that the three men did not act deliberately in combination with each other does not matter as the Court of Appeal has held that for the purposes of this section it was not necessary for a person to act deliberately in combination with at least two others present at the scene, but that it is sufficient that at least three people are present, each separately using or threatening unlawful violence (*R* v *NW* [2010] EWCA Crim 404), making answer B incorrect. The offence can be committed by using or threatening violence so HARLOW's conduct would be caught. The fact that the violence used by GREEN was towards property does not mean anything when considering violent disorder (it is only s. 3 affray where this plays a part), so answers C and D are incorrect.

General Police Duties, para. 3.9.4

139. Answer **B** — The initial period for a s. 60AA authorisation can last a maximum of 24 hours, making answer A incorrect. There is no power to stop and search persons and/or vehicles attached to a s. 60AA authorisation, making answer C incorrect. Once the initial authorisation period has ended, the power can be extended for a further 24 hours by an officer of the rank of superintendent or above, making answer D incorrect.

General Police Duties, para. 3.1.4

140. Answer **B** — Answer A is incorrect as people who have a disability, *or have had a disability in the past*, are protected against discrimination. Answer C is incorrect as people who are not married or civil partners do not have this characteristic but the Marriage (Same Sex Couples) Act 2013 extended marriage to same-sex couples and the Civil Partnership (Opposite-sex Couples) Regulations 2019 extended civil partnership to opposite-sex couples (they do have this characteristic). Answer D is incorrect as 'ethnic group' may include any group with a shared culture or history (*Mandla* v *Dowell Lee* [1983] 2 AC 548). Sikhs (*Mandla* v *Dowell Lee* [1983] 2 AC 548), Jewish people (*Seide* v *Gillette Industries Ltd* [1980] IRLR 427), Romany Gypsies (*Commission for Racial Equality* v *Dutton* [1989] QB 783) and Irish Travellers (*O'Leary* v *Allied Domecq Inns Ltd* (CL 950275 July 2000, Central London County Court)) have all been held to be ethnic groups, but Scots, Welsh and English are however *not* ethnic groups (*Dawkins* v *Department of the Environment* [1993] IRLR 284). Answer B is therefore the correct answer. Section 10(2) of the Equality Act 2010 (religion and belief) states that belief means any religious or philosophical belief and a reference to belief includes a reference to a lack of belief. The criteria for determining what is a 'philosophical belief' are that it must be genuinely held; be a belief and not an opinion or viewpoint based on the present state of information available; be a belief as to a weighty and substantial aspect of human life and behaviour; attain a certain level of cogency, seriousness, cohesion and importance; and be worthy of respect in a democratic society, compatible with human dignity and not conflict with the fundamental rights of others. For example, a belief in 'climate change' affecting how a person lived his/her life is protected by the Act (*Grainger plc* v *Nicholson* [2010] 2 All ER 253). A philosophical belief would only be excluded for failing to satisfy *Grainger plc* if it was the kind of belief the expression of which would be akin to Nazism or totalitarianism. The claimant held gender-critical beliefs, which included the belief that sex is immutable and not to be conflated with gender identity. Some transgender people found the claimant's remarks offensive and 'transphobic'. The tribunal held that the complainant's beliefs were widely shared and did not seek to destroy the rights of trans persons. The claimant's belief, whilst offensive to some, and notwithstanding its potential to result in the harassment of trans persons in some circumstances, fell within the protection under Article 9 of the ECHR and therefore was in line with s. 10 of the Equality Act 2010 (*Forstater* v *CGD Europe* [2021] UKEAT 0105 20 1006).

General Police Duties, paras 3.16.3.3, 3.16.3.4 to 3.16.3.6

141. Answer **C** — The Licensing Act 1872, s. 12 states:

> Every person found drunk in any highway or other public place, whether a building or not, or on any licensed premises, shall be liable ...

The offence is not limited to being found drunk on licensed premises, meaning that answer D is incorrect. It includes being found drunk 'on any licensed premises' meaning that answer B is incorrect. The offence has been held to apply to a licensee when found drunk on the licensed premises, even when those premises were not open to the public (*Evans* v *Fletcher* (1926) 135 LT 153) so both men commit the offence (correct answer C) and this means that answer A is incorrect.

General Police Duties, para. 3.6.4

142. Answer **D** — Section 62A creates two situations in which the power to direct people to leave land can be exercised: *one excluding the element at s. 62(2)(d) and one including it.* The table below illustrates the relevant circumstances; in order for a direction to be given under s. 62A, the senior officer present at the scene must have a reasonable belief that:

Situation 1 at least two people are trespassing on the land; and	Situation 2 at least two people are trespassing on the land; and
↓	↓
that they have at least one vehicle between them; and	that they have at least one vehicle between them; and
↓	↓
that they are there with the common purpose of residing there for any period; and	that they are there with the common purpose of residing there for any period; and
↓	↓
that the occupier (or person acting on the occupier's behalf) has asked the police to remove the trespassers from the land.	it appears to the officer that the person has one or more caravans in his possession or under his control on the land that there are relevant caravan sites with suitable pitches available for the trespassers to move to; and
	↓
	that the occupier (or person acting on the occupier's behalf) has asked the police to remove the trespassers from the land.

HODGSON is the only person trespassing so a s. 62A direction could not be given in this situation (correct answer D).

General Police Duties, para. 3.5.6

143. Answer **C** — Regulation 8 provides that if a member of a police force or a relative included in his/her family proposes to have, or has, a 'business interest', the member shall forthwith give written notice of that interest to the chief officer of police unless that business interest was disclosed at the time of the officer's appointment as a member of the force.

If a business interest is felt to be incompatible, the chief officer may dispense with the member's services after giving him/her an opportunity to make representations. Regulation 7(2) provides that a member of a police force or relative has a business interest if:

- the member holds any office or employment for hire or gain or carries on any business;
- the member or a relative of the member has a pecuniary interest in any licence or permit granted in relation to alcohol licensing, refreshment houses or betting and gaming or regulating places of entertainment in the area of the police force in question.

'Relative' means a spouse or civil partner who is not separated from the member, a person living with the member as if they were their spouse or civil partner, or a parent, son, daughter, brother or sister who is included in the member's family. LEEDHAM and PC REED's father would be 'relatives' and the nature of the business interest would be covered by the Regulations making answers A, B and D incorrect.

General Police Duties, para. 3.18.16.2

144. Answer **D** — The Terrorism Act 2000, s. 33 states:

(1) An area is a cordoned area for the purposes of this Act if it is designated under this section.
(2) A designation may be made only if the person making it considers it expedient for the purposes of a terrorist investigation.
(3) If a designation is made orally, the person making it shall confirm it in writing as soon as is reasonably practicable.

Section 33(3) states that the designation can be given orally (making answer C incorrect).

The Terrorism Act 2000, s. 34 states:

(1) Subject to subsections (1A), (1B) and (2), a designation under section 33 may only be made—
  (a) where the area is outside Northern Ireland and is wholly or partly within a police area, by an officer for the police area who is of at least the rank of superintendent, and
  (b) ...
(1A) ...
(1B) ...
(1C) ...
(2) A constable who is not of the rank required by subsection (1) may make a designation if he considers it necessary by reason of urgency.
(3) Where a constable makes a designation in reliance on subsection (2) he shall as soon as is reasonably practicable—
  (a) make a written record of the time at which the designation was made, and
  (b) ensure that a police officer of at least the rank of superintendent is informed.
(4) An officer who is informed of a designation in accordance with subsection (3)(b)—
  (a) shall confirm the designation or cancel it with effect from such time as he may direct, and
  (b) shall, if he cancels the designation, make a written record of the cancellation and the reason for it.

Section 34(1)(a) states that the designation will normally be made by an officer who is of at least the rank of superintendent (making answers A and B incorrect). However, in an urgent situation a constable can make the designation (s. 34(2)). If that is the case, the officer will inform an officer of the rank of superintendent or above as soon as reasonably practicable.

General Police Duties, paras 3.15.7 to 3.15.7.2

145. Answer **D** — Section 15(7) of PACE84 states that two copies shall be made of a warrant which specifies only one set of premises and does not authorise multiple entries; and as many copies as are reasonably required may be made of any other kind of warrant. This means that answers A, B and C are incorrect and that answer D is correct.

General Police Duties, para. 3.2.4

146. Answer **B** — Answer C is incorrect as an authorisation under s. 47A of the Terrorism Act 2000 authorises any constable in uniform to stop a vehicle in the specified area or place and to search:

(a) the vehicle;
(b) the driver of the vehicle;
(c) a passenger in the vehicle;
(d) anything in or on the vehicle or carried by the driver or a passenger.

Answer D is incorrect as a constable in uniform may exercise the power conferred by an authorisation only for the purpose of discovering whether there is anything which may constitute evidence that the vehicle concerned is being used for the purposes of terrorism or (as the case may be) that the person concerned is a terrorist within the meaning of s. 40 (s. 47A(4)). However, the power conferred by such an authorisation may be exercised whether or not the constable reasonably suspects that there is such evidence (s. 47A(5)).

PC BUCHANAN correctly stopped the vehicle and also correctly arrested SNOOKS (answer A is incorrect, answer B is correct) as the Terrorism Act 2000, s. 41(1) states that a constable may arrest without a warrant a person whom he/she reasonably suspects to be a terrorist.

General Police Duties, paras 3.15.6.1, 3.15.6.4

147. Answer **D** — Section 34 of the Anti-social Behaviour, Crime and Policing Act 2014 provides a dispersal power enabling officers (constables in uniform and police community support officers (PCSOs)) to direct a person who has committed, or is likely to commit, anti-social behaviour to leave a specified area and not return for a specified period of up to 48 hours (answers B and C are therefore incorrect). Answer A is incorrect as the direction would in most instances be given in writing to ensure that those individuals being dispersed are clear where they are being dispersed from. Where this is not reasonably practicable, *the direction could be given orally* (s. 35(5)(a)) and the officer would keep a written record of the direction (s. 38). The dispersal power can only be used where an officer of at least the rank of inspector has authorised its use in a specified locality (s. 34(1)). That authorisation can only be given where the police officer of or above the rank of inspector reasonably believes that, in respect of any locality within their police area, the exercise of the dispersal powers in part 3 of the Act may be required in order to remove or reduce the likelihood of the anti-social behaviour occurring (correct answer D).

General Police Duties, paras 3.7.6 to 3.7.6.2

148. Answer **D** — Section 7(2) of the Road Traffic Act 1988 states that a requirement under s. 7 to provide evidential breath specimens can be made:

(a) at a police station;
(b) at a hospital; or
(c) at or near a place where a preliminary breath test has been administered to that person or would have been but for his/her failure to cooperate with it.

The requirement for the specimen can be made at any of these locations (meaning that answers A and B are incorrect); 'other medical premises' are not included in s. 7(2) meaning that answer C is incorrect.

General Police Duties, para. 3.22.5.2

149. Answer **B** — Answer A is incorrect as an adult may be removed to, kept at or taken to a place of safety that is a police station but only in circumstances specified in the Mental Health Act 1983 (Places of Safety) Regulations 2017 (SI 2017/1036). Regulation 2(1) states:

An adult ('A') may only be removed to, kept at, or taken to, a place of safety that is a police station in the exercise of a power to which section 136A of the Act applies (4) where—

(a) the decision-maker is satisfied that—
    (i) the behaviour of A poses an imminent risk of serious injury or death to A, or to another person,

(ii) because of that risk, no place of safety other than a police station in the relevant police area can reasonably be expected to detain A, and
(iii) the requirement in sub-paragraph (b) of regulation 4(1) will be met, and
(b) where the decision-maker is not an officer of the rank of inspector or above, an officer of that rank or above authorises that A may be removed to, kept at, or taken to a place of safety that is a police station.

Regulation 2 further provides that where the person considering using a police station as a place of safety is a police officer, they must, if reasonably practicable, consult with a registered medical practitioner, a registered nurse, an approved mental health professional, an occupational therapist or a paramedic before making the decision. The decision to use a police station as a place of safety must be authorised by an officer of the rank of inspector or above (correct answer B). Answer D is incorrect as anyone being taken to a place of safety or detained at such a place will be treated as being in legal custody (s. 137(1)). This expression is only relevant in relation to escaping and assisting in an escape; it is very different from 'in police detention' used under s. 118 of PACE84.

Answer C is incorrect as a person removed to or kept at a place of safety under this section may be detained there for the permitted period of detention for the purpose of enabling him/her to be examined by a registered medical practitioner and to be interviewed by an approved mental health professional and of making any necessary arrangements for his/her treatment or care. The Mental Health Act 1983, s. 136 states:

(2A) In subsection (2), 'the permitted period of detention' means—
(a) the period of 24 hours beginning with—
(i) in a case where the person is removed to a place of safety, the time when the person arrives at that place;
(ii) in a case where the person is kept at a place of safety, the time when the constable decides to keep the person at that place; or
(b) where an authorisation is given in relation to the person under section 136B, that period of 24 hours and such further period as is specified in the authorisation.

General Police Duties, para. 3.4.2

150. Answer **A** — When an authorisation under s. 60 of the Criminal Justice and Public Order Act 1994 is given, you automatically get the powers provided by s. 60AA. So in addition to s. 60 powers, such an authorisation also allows officers *in uniform* to require any individual to remove any item (e.g. clothing, mask, scarf) if the officer reasonably believes that the person is wearing it/will wear it wholly or mainly to conceal his/her identity (this makes answers B and D incorrect). It is an offence to fail to remove such items when required to do so (s. 60AA(7)).

Therefore, PC MAKIN could use the power (making answer C incorrect). Note that this is not a power to stop and search a person for items that could be used to conceal their identity; it is only a power to stop a person and make the requirement to remove the item (making answer D further incorrect).

General Police Duties, para. 3.1.4